For Rabbi Nina this book which owes its existence to her, (in spite of the mother "only half listening")

The Wanderings of Isaac André Gedalia

A memoir

with gratitude

Sylvie Weil

PO Box 271
Marlboro VT 05344

SYLVIE WEIL

The Wanderings of Isaac André Gedalia

Translated by Ros Schwartz

IPBooks Infinite Possibilities
New York • http://www.IPBooks.net

The Wanderings of Isaac André Gedalia

Published by IPBooks, Queens, NY
Online at IPBooks.net

Original French title: *Les pérégrinations d'Isaac André Guédalia*

Copyright © 2025 by Sylvie Weil
English translation © 2025 by Ros Schwartz

All rights reserved. No part of this book may be used or reproduced in any manner whatsoever, including internet usage, without permission of the author and the translator.

Cover: Joshua Distler
Cover photo: Sylvie Weil
Thanks to Em Pinsan for the bubble

ISBN: 978-1-956864-90-8

For Eric

And for Nicolas who wanted to name him Curtis

Acknowledgment

I wish to thank Professor Nobuko Inaba for her helpful reading of the Japan chapters.

"You wonder what He's thinking of, Him up above," old Joe had said. "First He allows Auschwitz, and now this." *This* was thirty-four years ago.

Now I'm a bubble, barely bigger than a ping-pong ball, white and translucent, a little flame floating among other bubble-like white candles, other little flames, in a big silvery basin. My mother comes towards me and calls me by my name. We are reunited, she and I, truly reunited, officially reunited for the first time in thirty-four years. She repeats my name. She sheds a few tears, but not from sadness, more from a sort of happiness. There is such a thing as sad happiness.

What happened that evening was strictly between her and me. We were barely aware that others were present. Some twenty people, maybe a few more. Even so, my mother noticed two or three couples, still young, holding hands. She had come alone, after wavering for a long time. She had waited patiently for her turn to come up to the basin. From a distance, she had already picked me out among the others. She knew at once which one of those twenty or so identical round candles burning with tiny flames was me. Me, the one who was to be called Isaac André Gedalia. Quite a mouthful, people will say, especially for a translucent white bubble floating in a basin, but which could be explained. And which I shall explain.

The woman rabbi had given a lovely, very sensitive homily, mentioning that she too, et cetera. From the basin where I was floating, I could see that my mother was only half listening and couldn't care less. The only thing that interested her was me, the spherical little candle that she had recognized. I existed and she was about to call me by my name in front of witnesses.

My mother had never been the sort of person to join groups. That other women had lost babies was of no interest to her. She'd never felt the need to bond with them, to find out whether they had all experienced grief in the same way.

It was during a concert my parents were attending, at the exact moment when Peter Serkin was launching into Beethoven's Piano Sonata Opus 109, that I began to choke. I flailed around frantically because I was panicking and trying to get my breath back. My mother, poor thing, didn't realize what was happening to me. She said to herself: "My son's going to be a footballer, he's so agile, so strong." She thought it was funny. My kicks made her smile. "He's so energetic, so active!" I was choking to death.

When I stopped moving, she told herself that I was tired, that I was resting, that I was listening to the music, that I'd be a footballer who loved classical music. "Perhaps he's sucking his thumb," she thought. She'd read somewhere that fetuses suck their thumb in the womb and found that idea delightful and soothing. She loved that while she was listening to a beautiful concert, her baby too was doing something that gave him pleasure. Her baby was curled up over his dying heartbeats.

All night, she thought I was resting and that was why I was so still. She clung to that idea. My father put his face close to my mother's belly and called to me in a joking voice: "Listen, little Isaac, this is your daddy talking to you. Are you okay? Give us a little sign." It was the doctor who had to inform them that my heart had stopped beating.

The very next day, I was chucked into a hospital waste bin. No one had consulted my parents. Disappeared, Isaac André Gedalia. In actual fact, I had already taken leave of the tiny body that had been mine for seven months but which was no longer any use to anyone.

I may as well explain those three first names right away. Firstly, why Isaac? Because, on the morning when my father told my mother that she was pregnant, she reacted with disbelief like Sarah in the Bible. She laughed. She had been hoping for three years.

"No! You really think so? How can you tell?"

"Your skin. It feels different. Not only your skin. When I pinch you, it feels as if I'm pinching a sponge."

My mother burst out laughing.

"Are you sure?"

"He will be called Isaac," declared my father, a Bible lover. After that, whenever he spoke about me, it was always "Little Isaac."

Here's a reminder of the story for those who are less versed in biblical tales. Three passing travelers who were in fact angels informed Abraham that Sarah would give birth to a son. Sarah, who had overheard their conversation from the door of the tent where she was making cakes for the three visitors, began to laugh. She didn't believe it, she thought that she and Abraham were far too old. But the Eternal had already announced the news to Abraham some time earlier, and he had fallen flat on his face, also laughing, and said to himself: "To a man who is one hundred years old, a son will be born? With Sarah who is ninety?" Then God said to him: "You will call him Yitzhak," which in Hebrew means "he will laugh." Who was supposed to laugh? The child? My parents weren't old and my mother was laughing with delight. Incredulous because this news was such a great joy.

I would also be called André in honor of my maternal grandfather, who my mother secretly hoped I would take after. He had been handsome in his youth, a thin face, curly jet-black hair, a well-defined mouth, round tortoiseshell spectacles—the epitome of the European intellectual. He was a famous French mathematician and I'd have met him, of course, had I been born. I shan't say much about him because he has already been talked about a great deal. And lastly, I would be called Gedalia in honor of my paternal great grandfather, who wasn't at all famous but was still a character: very pious, passionate about pickles and wrestling. He made wine in his cellar and was adored by my father. My mother hadn't known him but she'd taken him to her heart when, barely arrived from France, she'd married my father and moved to the Bronx, a place she'd never heard of before.

Here I'll digress for a moment: I was thrilled to have as my parents two enthusiastic people who, on listening to Peruvian music a few days after they met, had decided to set off at once to go live in the Andes and wait tables in a cheap eatery and have lots of children who would speak Quechua. I would have spoken Quechua! They didn't get very far, only to an annex of the Bronx city hall where they hastily tied the knot. As for Gedalia, a scrawny old man with a long face and dark eyes, come from Ukraine to Brooklyn via Canada, curiously he had become part of my mother's day-to-day life. My father looked like him, a striking resemblance according to the family. The same dark eyes, black hair, not to mention the same sense of humor. One day, when she was clearing out a cupboard to make room for her belongings, my mother discovered a large prayer shawl of beautiful white wool, only slightly moth-eaten, slightly yellowed, with wide black stripes and carefully knotted fringes. She shook it out and spread it in the sun. She was the self-appointed custodian of her new but departed grandfather's tallith. She would talk to me of this grandfather as she aired his prayer shawl, saying: "Maybe you'll take after him too." That idiosyncratic and very religious ancestor who should have been mine had left Ukraine in 1912, having survived a pogrom. He'd been alerted by a peasant who took part in that pogrom but had a soft spot for the Jew Gedalia. Gedalia hid in his cellar for three days with his wife and daughters, giving the girls wine to drink so they would sleep and not cry. In Canada, where he emigrated initially, he bought a farm. He'd been forced to uproot the family due to the lack of Jewish husbands for his four daughters. So he transported them all to Brooklyn, which was teeming with Jewish husbands and where he built up a thriving grocery store. After having sold countless marinated herrings, smoked salmon, pickles and other specialties, he died some twenty years before my mother and father met.

According to an ancient Jewish tradition, the soul of a child that has just died flutters around like a bird for a few days, finding it hard to say goodbye to its parents and its home. That was true for me, even though I wasn't yet born. In medieval times, when a little Jewish child died, the family was careful to leave the window wide open (if they had one, otherwise the door), so that the child's soul could come and go. They believed that when it felt ready to fly away once and for all, angels would come to fetch it and accompany it to Gan Eden—Paradise—where it would play and study alongside other children.

I wasn't ready yet. In any case, the windows of the hospital where I wasn't born didn't open. But I didn't flutter around, I limited myself to following my mother everywhere, or rather clinging to her, to her clothes, her skin, which isn't very difficult for a little soul. I wanted to remain a part of her life for a little while longer. I knew that she could sense my presence and that that gave her some comfort.

No one had imagined for one moment that little Isaac André Gedalia, having spent long months rather uneventfully snuggled in the warmth of a cozy, happy womb, would suffer convulsions while his parents were listening to Peter Serkin playing a Beethoven sonata, and that he'd never come into the world. Two days after she came home from the hospital, my father took my mother to see a big orchid show at the Bronx Botanical Garden, close to where they lived. To take her mind off things. He couldn't have foreseen that she would develop an abiding horror of orchids. She found them grotesque, venomous, threatening. What's more, she very quickly lost interest in the show. On the other hand, she was fascinated by the babies in strollers. She would even go up to them, in the grip of a crazy—truly crazy when you think about it— urge to tell their mothers that she too would soon need a stroller. That she wanted one that was robust but not too heavy. She almost went so far as to ask them whether they recommended that particular brand, whether they were satisfied with it. Her addled brain hadn't yet grasped that there'd been a change of plan and that she would have no need for a stroller. She would not be wheeling a baby around in the New York spring. As for me, still hovering around her because I hadn't resigned myself to leaving her yet, I felt sorry for her.

"Little Isaac, my poor little darling," she'd say to me in her moments of lucidity, "you already existed and I loved you so much. Did you hear your father's sobs as he was putting away all the records he'd chosen to play for you in the womb? Bach, Mozart. He wanted you to come into the world immersed already in the most beautiful music. We did share those short, wonderful moments of happiness."

That's how my mother spoke to me. Softly. She kept speaking to me. She was right to sense that I was still close to her. I was there. Not anywhere else. Not yet.

Of course, I'd heard my father sobbing. I'd heard him reading the Book of Job aloud in the hush of night. But Job gets everything back eventually—his donkeys, his camels and his children. Apparently, that's not the true ending. Someone supposedly tacked on the happy end. As for me, already suffocated but still present, I very much wished I could sob too. I knew my parents' voices. I knew their slightest changes of intonation. No one has any idea how much a little one inside the womb can pick up. And that's even before the hearing faculty has fully developed. We lived in the Bronx, in an apartment building filled with old women. Their voices constantly rang through the hallways and rose up from the street in front of the building where they sat out all day long in folding chairs, weather permitting. It was like a hum. Each time my mother left our apartment, I listened out for that slightly jarring murmur; our old ladies' voices weren't very melodious. But that murmur soothed me as my mother exchanged pleasantries with her neighbors. A Russian hum, a Yiddish hum, ceaseless, sometimes whiny, memories of the days when the neighborhood was classier and the building better maintained, memories of Odessa from where they'd had to flee for a future in the Bronx they'd hoped would be better. Sometimes low but harsher voices speaking in hushed tones. Those were the memories of Auschwitz. There was one old voice in particular, a weary voice that never rose above a whisper, as if it didn't have the strength. That voice would often come close to my mother's ear saying just one sentence, never two: "They made us dance in the camps, you know." Then I would hear slow little footsteps receding. She and her husband lived on our floor. They were called Feinberg. I quickly understood that the people who had truly suffered spoke little and didn't whine.

My parents' voices tended to be cheerful, rarely grumpy. They weren't complainers. I recognized my future big brother's voice too. He was going on fifteen. His voice was deeper than my father's. He spoke more slowly and his English accent was a little different. He was excited about my arrival in the world and had chosen the name of a famous baseball player for me. "It would be much better than Isaac," he'd say. "More modern." He spoke French with my mother. I was going to be born into a multilingual family.

The Wanderings Of Isaac André Gedalia

There's a story I'm particularly keen to tell. A story that confirmed that the life awaiting me would certainly not be boring, and even that I was highly likely to have fun.

This big brother, who I already thought of as mine, had taken a job as a pizza delivery boy. Every afternoon, as soon as he'd finished his homework, he'd spend a couple of hours delivering pizzas for a small neighborhood Italian pizzeria. Friendly, polite, delivering his pizzas in all weather, undeterred either by driving rain or blizzards, he earned very good tips. He saved up all his money to buy himself a huge boom box, which was a fad among the youth of the early 1980s. The day finally came when he and my father went to choose one. And the magnificent, brand-new object the size of a small suitcase was set up in his bedroom. My brother was over the moon. I could hear his exclamations, and the music, too. He was into hip-hop. Two weeks later, no more hip-hop. An ominous silence. My brother had let himself be persuaded to lend his beloved boom box to a local guy, who'd promised to return it very quickly. Only he didn't return it and gave no further sign of life.

In our neighborhood there were loads of youngsters from different backgrounds—Irish, Italian, Albanian,

Russian. They hung out in groups who saw themselves as proper little gangs. My big brother had become friendly with the Russians. They were the most recent arrivals, like him and my mother. They came from Russia or Ukraine, my brother from France. To be "fresh off the boat" creates an immediate bond. The boy who had borrowed the boom box was an Irish kid, whose ear, according to my brother, was adorned with a crucifix that stretched the lobe out of all proportion. My brother wasn't able to find him, even though he lived nearby and people knew him. So, one Sunday morning, my parents got into their car and drove around the neighborhood, stopping every now and then to ask if anyone had seen the young man or if they knew where he could be found. They were so supportive, those parents, trawling the neighborhood in their little red Toyota in search of the boy who'd borrowed, or perhaps pinched—it was okay to surmise—my future brother's boom box. As for me, in my mother's womb, somewhat shaken up by my father's abrupt turns, I gave little kicks to show that I was participating fully in this pursuit, that they had my support. My mother responded by patting her belly.

They came home empty-handed, but word had already spread around the neighborhood that these young, determined parents were looking for a fight. Then the borrower's clan started arming themselves with iron bars in preparation for a rumble, a good old street fight. Between gangs, between real gangs, the rumble was seen as the normal way to resolve a problem.

My future parents, who'd given up the hunt and parked their Toyota, had no inkling. They'd barely finished lunch when a strange procession began. There was a ring at the door, my mother opened it and at once I heard a booming, youthful voice with a strong Russian accent: "I'm Igor. If you need me, you'll find me at the ice cream store." Five minutes later, another ring at the door. It was a certain Sasha who, in a splendid bass voice, solemnly offered his services, and then Yuri… They too would wait for the signal at the ice cream store. It belonged to a Ukrainian whose tiny shop was a meeting place. I heard all those beautiful voices resounding somewhere above me and I laughed. I told myself that life in this family wasn't going to be dull. They were dream parents, those two, and my brother had the most amazing luck. Luck that I wanted to share, luck that was ultimately denied me.

Yes, truly, fate, or rather the demon that had the idea of sending me out into the cold while waiting for a possible return to Gan Eden, committed a terrible injustice. A crime. People will say, of course, that it's the demons' specialty—their mission, even—and that it would be mistaken to expect anything else from them. But even so. That's what old Joe had clearly understood. That it was a crime.

Who was old Joe? Joseph, known as Joe, was a survivor of Auschwitz and Bergen-Belsen. He lived opposite us and his low, slightly sharp voice had become familiar. He spoke more or less in a monotone. What's more, he said little, confining himself to the essential. No flourishes, no unnecessary words. His only son had been killed by an SS who had swung him by the feet and smashed his head against a wall. Joe proudly recounted how the SS had had to bang him several times to finish him off.

"That's how strong he was, my son, and he wasn't even two years old. The child's mother was killed on the spot by a bullet through the back of her head. That was the best thing that could have happened to her."

"Stop it, Joseph," his wife, fat Selma, would interrupt him. "That's enough now. You don't want to upset her with all those horror stories, especially not now."

Then Joe would put on his hat.

"Ladies, I leave you to have your conversation."

"That's right, Joe, go for your walk."

I knew Selma's voice well because my mother often used to go and spend time with her. How did I know she was fat? Her voice. Resonant, cheerful and comfortable. Voices aren't deceptive. Selma's voice was round. Besides, Selma herself was forever saying that she was fat. She was proud of it. It was like a vengeance, a victory over the skeletal past of her adored Joseph. She loved food. She plied my mother with fortifying broths, and also cakes.

"You must eat," she'd say. "Especially now."

"Especially now," echoed the old ladies who spent their days sitting in the street outside the building, enjoying the mild spring weather and the sun that did their old bones so much good. They kept an eye on the comings and goings, and nothing escaped them. "Don't run, be careful, don't take any risks, especially now."

Towards the end of winter, my presence had become noticeable. My mother would stroke her belly with satisfaction and whisper to me: "Do you hear that, little Isaac? They're all watching out for us."

She liked to go and sit in a nearby park next to the highway. My mother would watch the stream of cars heading north, towards the verdant, wealthy suburbs. She'd say to me: "You see, they're leaving, but we're staying put. It's good to be one of those who stay, who don't go anywhere. Your mother is a mussel clinging to the shore, a limpet wedded to her rock. It's a change for me," she'd add, laughing. "You have a mother who has moved a thousand times in her life! A mother who's been scattered about."

My mother was indeed scattered about. With a mother like that, I would probably never have known exactly who I was. I was slowly taking on a human form in the Bronx, but I already belonged in very different places: I crawled on the grass in a tiny square garden with a pear tree in the center, and that tree produced delicious pears which had once been the pride of the woman who'd have been my great-grandmother. The little garden was in the village in the Sarthe where she had lived during World War II. As a child, my mother spent all her holidays there, and so did my big brother. I also had my ride booked on a pony that went around the pond in the Luxembourg Gardens in Paris. There too, I had my special seat on the white elephant on the merry-go-round. Or on the giraffe. My so-called heritage went in all directions. I'd have spent my life asking myself questions. But what does it matter? I would have been the adored child of a scattered-about mother, and that's it.

One day, we had just come out of the building to go for a walk and I was troubled by an unusual racket: all around me, the old women were yapping:

"Tell him to buy you a bed, it's the least he can do!"

"Sleeping on a mattress on the floor, the idea! Especially now!" And my mother's voice, laughing and gentle:

"Perhaps Max forgot to mention there was a box spring under the mattress?"

"A box spring isn't a bed! You have to tell him… tell him…" retorted the chorus.

What was that about? The old ladies weren't the only ones to be excited, reinvigorated by the coming spring: apparently the ants were also reinvigorated and excited and had invaded the building. So, one morning, when my father was out, my mother called Max, a former trucker, a giant with tiny, very blue eyes lost in a fat, jovial face who was bored stiff since giving up his truck. He was the strong man, the Samson, of our little tribe, and my mother asked him to move some furniture in her bedroom to get rid of the ants. "He's got piggy eyes," my mother whispered to me. It was her nature to make fun of people and she would share her impressions with me. "You, little Isaac, you won't have piggy eyes."

"Tell him... tell him..." Once they got started, our elderly neighbors were unstoppable.

"Him" was my father, of course. The man. Who definitely owed his lawful wife a proper bed.

"Especially now," echoed the chorus. "Especially now."

I liked those two words, it was like a message addressed to me personally, all day long. Sometimes it even felt as if that was my name. I was called Especially Now and I was famous in a Bronx neighborhood. I had learned to make out the voices surrounding my mother that spoke those two words in very different accents. Russian, Yiddish and also the nasal and rather unattractive Bronx accent. There was a man with a distinguished voice who didn't say much but never missed an opportunity to say: "Don't run, don't run" and contented himself with adding: "There's no point." His voice wasn't young but was pleasant on the ear, as if smiling. That was Mr. Ruben. That's what everyone always called him. I don't know what his first name was. From what I gathered, he wasn't a refugee from anywhere, and he'd been the first person to move into the building as soon as it was finished. The old ladies never spoke his name without adding that he was "a true gentleman."

Sam, my future paternal grandfather, was probably the person who was most thrilled about my imminent arrival. Having learned that his daughter-in-law was expecting a boy, he had immediately announced that a boy was wonderful! He would have said the same thing if he'd learned that I was to be a girl. That's what he was like. When my parents went out to eat in a restaurant with Sam and Molly, my future grandmother, I would invariably hear Sam exclaim enthusiastically that he'd never tasted a better soup, chop or chips.

And he'd announced at once that he would teach his grandson to play the saxophone.

"For a boy, the saxophone is the best instrument, it's character-forming, it builds confidence," Sam would say. He loved giving lengthy explanations. "The saxophone is relatively recent, invented in 1843 by a Belgian clarinetist called Antoine-Joseph 'Adolphe' Sax. Sax put a wooden mouthpiece with a simple reed inside the body of a brass instrument. That is why the saxophone is a brass instrument that belongs to the woodwind family. The richest sound is that of the alto saxophone, which carries the tune while the other instruments provide harmonizations. People are afraid of taking it up, they say: 'My lungs aren't powerful enough, I don't have enough puff, I wouldn't be able to play.' But they're wrong. Puff comes from playing. On the other hand, you need nimble fingers, whether for the saxophone or the clarinet."

Sam's soft, slightly husky voice was one of my favorite voices. His southwestern drawl lulled me, I felt good, I dozed, I dreamed, I hoped to have nimble fingers so I'd be able to start playing the saxophone the day I was born. The next day at the latest.

Sam had grown up in Colorado where his parents, Galitzianers who'd come from the Austro-Hungarian empire, had gone to live on their arrival in America. Sam's father, Tzvi-Hersch, was a tailor. My father knew nothing else about them, neither where exactly they came from nor what their life had been like back there.

When Sam had arrived in New York, holding his saxophone in one hand and his modest belongings in the other, he had just celebrated his twentieth birthday. He planned to become a saxophonist. But it was just at the time of the Great Depression. He had to eat. The young Sam sold his precious instrument. During the months when I was part of the family, so to speak, I heard a lot about that saxophone which he had never stopped lamenting.

The voice of Molly, my paternal grandmother, was very different from her husband's: loud, jarring, not at all smooth like Selma's. It was a voice that jolted you awake, even when Molly was trying to be pleasant. Her usual way of expressing herself was in a volley of reprimands and recriminations. The first time I heard her voice, I was more violently shaken up than I ever had been in the little red Toyota: "What? Potato salad without onions? What's this all about, am I expected to change all my recipes? The recipes handed down to me by my beloved Mama, may she rest in peace. She would bite into an onion as if it was an apple, I can still see her..." And what had set off that shrill outburst? My future mother had asked for onions not to be put in some dishes because the smell made her nauseous.

Molly would drop in every so often to see "us." She'd inspect the place, poking her nose into the cupboards and the fridge, and she found that while my mother organized the dishes properly, she didn't do the housework often enough. "So, my grandson will be crawling around in the dust?" she'd exclaim, noisily indignant as always, but it was her way of showing that she was happy at the thought of being a grandmother, and I detected the hint of a smile in her voice.

My four grandparents never met. My parents had decided that those four characters, endowed with such different personalities, would have nothing in common.

My maternal grandparents spoke French. I didn't hear much of them because they didn't live in New York. André, the mathematician, had a voice that sounded a little heavy, slightly drawling, with intonations that came to him from

Antwerp and Strasbourg, and also from Vienna and Rostov-on-Don. He spoke slowly, emphasizing each syllable, and would sometimes burst out laughing, a big laugh that was a joy to hear.

My grandmother Eveline had a clear, musical voice, which sounded playful and very pretty even when she said things that my mother thought were not particularly nice, for example: "Can you see me in the Luxembourg Gardens or any other Parisian garden, standing by the sandbox or the swings, calling out: "Isaac, come and eat your snack!" Of course, she'd have preferred Pierre, Paul or François. But I was much too colorful a little soul for that kind of name.

All the same, my two grandmothers did have one thing in common: they both loved the foxtrot, which they'd practiced a great deal in their young days, one in Paris, the other in Brooklyn, but they never had the opportunity to gratify the family with a little dance number together!

By the way, how did the story of the boom box borrowed but not returned end? My parents made it known that they had no wish to fight, only to recover what belonged to them. A meeting was organized at the corner of a certain street. The borrower, boom box perched on his shoulder, arrived flanked by a few young Irish bodyguards. My brother walked slowly towards him, escorted by a number of Sashas, Igors and Dimas. My parents followed at a distance. The object was restored to its rightful owner and everyone went home.

Yes, little Isaac, those hours I spent alone with you watching the cars streaming towards the northern suburbs were blessed hours. I'd tell you everything that went through my mind. I'd tell you that it's good to be one of the people who stay, who don't go anywhere. In the families you would have been descended from, the idea of staying somewhere, staying for good, was more a dream than a reality. And yes, you would have been the beloved child of a scattered-about mother.

I'd joke with you, stroking my belly. Caressing you. I'd tell you that you could be proud of a very varied heritage, a real patchwork. Can one speak of a harlequin heritage? I'd then launch into a detailed enumeration of the disparate elements of what I called your heritage.

It began with the tiger skin and the gong brought back from Tonkin by your great-grandfather, whom nobody had ever known because he died in 1914. Your mother and her cousins rolled around on that tiger skin throughout their childhood. We merrily banged away on that gong, which was used to beat out the steps of those condemned to death on their way to be executed.

And then the saxophone, of course. Like your father, you'd have grown up with that saxophone sold by Sam during the Great Depression of 1929. This instrument would have been part of your life. How come, since it had been sold? Because your grandfather Sam would have told you about the saxophone the very day you were born, and the next day and the day after that.

Then there are two grimacing Mexican masks in black lacquered wood, with big teeth that are the real fangs of some animal or other. I've always seen them on a shelf in your grandfather André's office. To greet the children who come to see him in his office, André hurriedly hides his face behind the scariest of his two masks and lets out terrifying roars. You'd have played the game, like all of us before you: you'd have screamed and pretended to be very frightened.

The barn door of a small and very old house in a village in the Sarthe. Back home. Two words so easy to slide into. You'd have loved the sounds you hear back home. The creak of the door when you swing on it, eyes closed, the warmth of the midday sun on your face. The loud, coarse voices of the men who sit down to lunch in the neighboring houses, windows wide open. The dying hum of a wasp drowning in a puddle of cider on the green gingham waxed tablecloth. The women with their broad smiles who ask: "Feels good to be home, doesn't it?" And the big loaves of farmhouse bread from which they carve generous slices.

The broken silver candlestick, repaired and religiously handed down in your father's family. Lest we forget. What mustn't we forget? The day and the night that your ancestors Schmiel-Haïm and Esther, Gedalia's parents, Molly's grandparents, spent locked in their cellar with their youngest children while overhead men shouted, swore and smashed cupboards with rifle butts and boots. On the 18th of October 1905, "they" entered Schmiel-Haïm's house in Uman. Angry not to find any Jews to lay their hands on, or perhaps, on the contrary, greatly relieved—who can say?—because much less bloodthirsty than craving good alcohol and loot, "they" began by drinking all the wine set aside by Schmiel-Haïm for the Sabbath. Then one of them grabbed the candlestick and, finding it too light, smashed the meager loot against his boot and threw it to the ground. Shmiel-Haim carefully glued it back together.

A bridge crossed in 1941. Over a flat, dark river, this is the bridge crossed for all eternity—at least for the eternity of our family—by a girl called Maryse, along with an elderly woman, a much younger woman, and a little boy. At either end of the bridge, a white barrier. On one side a German sentry box, on the other a tricolored sentry box, a world that is still French: the Free Zone. Every ten meters, a German sentry. Maryse, the heroine of your prehistory as well as mine, makes the introductions: *Meine Mutter, meine Schwester, mein Neffe.* Heart pounding, the fake mother and sister have to shake hands with the sentries. They try to stop their hands from trembling in those of the steely-eyed Germans. Your great-grandmother and your grandmother Eveline. The same one you've no doubt heard complaining at the idea of taking a child named Isaac for a walk in the Luxembourg Gardens.

The samovar that André's grandmother, Hermine Solomonovna, took with her when she was forced to flee Rostov-on-Don with her husband, children, and all their belongings, driven out by what she understatedly called "a little breeze of anti-Semitism." This expression had become proverbial in the family. Your ancestor Hermine considered that a well-bred lady should never dwell on unpleasant topics. A pogrom was an unpleasant topic. She preferred to evoke pleasant memories, long sleigh rides "across the fairytale whiteness of the infinite steppes" and the hum of the samovar that greeted her in her well-heated house in Rostov.

Gedalia's "kemmerl." A small room that he had reserved for himself in the cellar of his building. This kemmerl had a bathtub, and the neighbors suspected your great-grandfather of trampling his grapes in it before fermenting them in barrels. No one ever saw him trample his grapes, but if he didn't trample them, how did he make his wine and what was the bathtub for? Once the wine was in the barrels, the grandfather didn't rest. Gedalia Shackman never rested. He even had a farm in Canada. Ah! The farm in Canada! A farm in Ontario around 1916 was no bed of roses and you would have heard all about it! It's the family's "Little House on the Prairie." Once his wine was in the barrels, your energetic forebear steeped cucumbers and peppers in large buckets filled with brine. Or he salted and marinated raw herring, as they do in Russia. Before eating the cucumbers and herrings, he would run them under the cold tap for hours. Why did he do this? Because his doctor forbade him from eating salty food. These are the tales and lore of your family. You smile and nod when you hear about Gedalia's kemmerl, you dream when you hear about the farm in Canada, and you laugh out loud when you hear about salted and desalted herrings. And then your father would tell you how he used to watch wrestling matches on TV with his religious, wrestling-mad grandfather, whose hero was the terrifying Killer Kowalski.

Your father's magnificent collection of Haggadahs: Haggadahs in Hebrew, in Yiddish, or according to the Sephardic rite. Haggadahs with variants and learned and esoteric commentaries, eighteenth-century Haggadahs written in Ladino, Haggadahs in French, Russian, Spanish and other languages, magnificent facsimiles of medieval Haggadahs, not to mention the four different translations he himself made of the Hebrew text.

Every year, while preparing his own multilingual and highly entertaining seder, your father would have told you about the seder of Gedalia, whose favorite grandson he was, naturally—the pious and highly educated grandson who, at the age of twelve, knew the prayers by heart and would easily be able to lead the service after the grandfather's death.

He would have told you how your great-grandfather, wearing a black skullcap and without his usual cigarette, sat at the head of the table, reading the Haggadah, reciting prayers and blessings faster and faster, his Hebrew sounding like Yiddish, and nobody understanding a word. But it didn't matter, it was both ridiculous and reassuring to see him doing everything exactly as it was done in the old country. The women kept chattering and when they made too much noise Gedalia would bang on the table and shout *Sha!* It all happened in Brooklyn, in the dining room of Gedalia and Rivka, your great-grandmother, in the red brick building where your father grew up. He would have described it all to you with such joy, so that it would always be part of your very own seder.

And then there's the pretty wooden dancer from Brazil on the table where André does his mathematics, which has been there ever since I can remember. Every so often, he would look up from his typewriter and spin his little dancer, with a light flick of his fingertips. And, like the children who came before you, under the watchful and fretful eye of your grandfather, you too would have held your breath as you delicately spun her around on her slender pedestal, intrigued by the precarious balance of the little dancer made of jacaranda wood.

One day, little Isaac, in New England, in an old rural cemetery I'd entered out of curiosity, my eyes were drawn to a grave, a very old little grave overgrown with moss, which was that of an eighteen-month infant. He had been run over by an oxcart. The epitaph made me cry. It seemed to me that I could hear the voice of the mother, still worried, eternally worried: she invoked the protection of the angels for her child because, the inscription said:

"He was much too little to go away all alone. He must be frightened."

And weren't you, Isaac André Gedalia, far too little to be left to fend for yourself? And what's more, thrown into a garbage bin?

I'm sitting on a sofa in a living room with two other women. All three of us are seven months pregnant. The other two are making plans—the birth, layette, names. I don't know how to tell them, without being disagreeable, that it doesn't concern me because the child I'm carrying is already dead. I end up telling them that I am so very sad.

It's a dream, of course, a tenacious dream that never misses an opportunity to invade my night. It's my inheritance, little Isaac, it's what you bequeathed me.

And then there are all the dreams that have nothing to do with you, and that I have to decipher and decode to understand that they lead me to you via circuitous, tortuous paths. The bizarre images, the tormented, tortured visions that haunt me at night lead me to you but I know perfectly well you are not the one sending them to me. Innocent little soul, you are in no way to blame for my grief. And no, you don't appear to me in these dreams. How could you? I was never given the opportunity to know your face. You were deprived of a face. All that remained was the idea engraved in me, imprinted somewhere on a secret retina, of a tiny face disfigured, destroyed, reduced to nothing, when you had to be extracted from me, from the shelter that my womb had been for a beautiful and happy future little Isaac.

Sometimes I see a horribly disfigured boy afflicted with a perpetual twisted smile. He holds in his hand a piece of paper on which are written fragments of words. I'm told he's been like this for seven years, and that he never lets go of his piece of paper. It's his talisman to guide him through life. When he was very young, he lost his parents in Auschwitz. The first thing they did was separate him and his mother from his father. At the last minute, the father took the child's face in his hand as he showed his wife a piece of paper on which he had written in red letters "To see your face one more time." The child grabbed the paper and it tore. A fragment remained in his hand and he never let go of it.

And then, there is this puny, ugly couple whom I find ridiculous, whom I hate and despise. They have a baby who is also sickly and ugly. I see him every day, sitting upright in his cot. His skin is of an indeterminate color, he looks like a scrawny cat. I start to love this baby because I remember that I myself lost a baby. I go into his parents' room to see the skinny, ugly child every time they go out. One day they come back and find the baby in my arms. I tell them it could well be mine.

And you have also left me that long moment that has stayed with me, when I felt you moving like never before and rejoiced in what I thought was life, when in fact it was death.

Should we have thought of amulets? Yes, that was it, no need to look any further. We'd forgotten the amulets. My future mother was a modern, enlightened young woman, an intellectual who hadn't thought of the amulets which her forebears would have considered essential. It hadn't occurred to her that the mazzikim, the demons, are jealous of human happiness. Most of all, they want to stop humans from reproducing, so they contrive to prevent marriages and are always on the lookout in a house where a woman is pregnant. They're ready to take advantage of the slightest lapse. My mother hadn't thought to protect herself and me against demons in general, and the dreaded Lilith in particular. I'm not even sure that grandfather Gedalia would have thought of that. His rabbi, a Hasid with a long ginger beard, would perhaps have recommended one or two, very discreetly.

I should have been the one to remember. I'd come from afar, I'd been around for a very long time, and I knew more about such things than my mother. But even if it had occurred to me, I don't know if I'd have been able to communicate to her that she should buy good amulets and surround herself with them, and that she should fix one, or several, at the head of her bed and wear one around her neck, and also that she should write on the walls of her room, clearly visible, the names of the three angels who were the only ones who could have protected us: Senoy, Sansenoy and Semangelof.

As for the amulets, there was no lack of choice. There are lots of them, and some very pretty ones. For example, a late seventeenth-century amulet made in Amsterdam depicts Adam and Eve on either side of a tree around which the legendary serpent is coiled. They're surrounded by beasts—a lion, a deer, a ram, a dog, and several other small animals, a cat, maybe, and something that looks like a mouse. The text reads: "Adam and Eve... Lilith be gone! Angels Senoy Sansenoy Semangelof... destroy Satan!" This is the most concise and common formula against Lilith, and probably the most effective.

My mother could have got hold of a copy. There's no reason why a copy shouldn't do just as well, as long as it's made, and most importantly engraved, with respect and accuracy by a professional who's very pious and sufficiently educated to do it exactly right. The mazzikim are clever, but not clever enough to see the difference between the seventeenth-century original and a quality copy, made towards the end of the twentieth century by a pious Jewish artist in Brooklyn or Jerusalem. What matters is the formula written in well-formed characters. A correct formula, even one copied onto a piece of cardboard, as long as it is exact and inscribed with proper respect, will not fail to scare away any demons who might attempt to come near.

A famous medieval manual made the following recommendation: "And to prevent a woman from miscarrying, write on the skin of a cat: 'Merciful King, have pity on this woman, that she may not miscarry the fruit with which she is pregnant, and keep away from her all the spirits, demons, devils and Liliths who will come to destroy and kill and corrupt and abort the child that is in her womb.'"

My mother-to-be was very fond of cats and I couldn't imagine her buying a cat skin to use as a talisman, even supposing that its effectiveness had been recognized and proven. Besides, where would she have found one in New York? On the other hand, she probably wouldn't have had too much trouble getting hold of a pretty amulet representing the three angels in the traditional way, that is as three fanciful-looking birds, each with its name inscribed on its body. And always, clearly visible, in large letters, the formula without which everything else is pointless: "Adam and Eve... Lilith be gone!"

So who is this Lilith who is commanded in no uncertain terms to leave the premises, all premises, this Lilith who is not welcome anywhere? It's time I spoke about her. But that's not easy. Because no human can claim to have seen her, really seen her, we don't know what she looks like. But those who know about demons say that she is a beautiful demoness with two large wings and magnificent long hair.

Some say that she kills newborns and also unborn children, others that she steals them and takes them with her (no one says where). Still others say she "steals the male child, drinks his blood, sucks his marrow and devours his flesh." Me, she didn't devour, she merely strangled me during a concert. I should count myself lucky.

Lilith was Adam's first wife, fashioned just like him but with impure earth, which explains her demonic character. Things didn't work out between her and Adam. They had no children. She fled to the shores of the Red Sea, where she frolicked with all sorts of demons. God sent three angels,

Senoy, Sansenoy and Semangelof, to bring her back but she refused to return. What happened next is less clear. Some say that to take revenge on Adam when he married Eve, she swore to kill as many of their descendants as possible. The three angels told her that all her children would die. To appease them, she swore not to harm the women and babies under their protection. In the meantime, she married a demon called Samael and gave birth to swarms of demons.

The amulets must therefore include the names of the three angels. Experts in the battle against demons recommend drawing the three angels with their wings, arms, legs... You can also decide to do things differently and flatter Lilith into sparing the newborn baby she's planning to attack. Apparently, what she likes most of all is to see her name beautifully engraved on the amulet, and especially her image with her superb hair spread around her. However, care is always taken to depict her surrounded by the three angels Senoy, Sansenoy and Semangelof.

Amulets depicting her in chains—a logical precaution—are probably only half-pleasing to her but are effective all the same. Naturally, for added security, she is surrounded by the three angels.

I did not behave as a coward. Quite the opposite, in fact. I was a brave baby. I fought Lilith valiantly and for as long as I could. How did I know it was her? What a question! Who else would have gone to such lengths to suffocate the innocent Isaac André Gedalia? Who else but that demoness whose passion is tearing babies away from their mothers, before or after birth, and killing them? She didn't tear me away, strictly speaking, but simply asphyxiated me. For the entire duration of a sonata, Lilith worked at suffocating me. That idiot Serkin was blithely playing his Beethoven and my mother was listening. I felt her hands gently resting on her belly, and therefore on me, her loving and gentle and protective hands which, at that moment when other cruel and implacable hands were strangling me, could do nothing for me. The hands of a mother who, even if she had understood what was happening, could only have been a helpless spectator to her baby's desperate struggle to live.

Why, oh why had no one thought of the amulets? A beautiful, large amulet hanging from a pretty gold chain or a velvet cord around the neck of my mother-to-be and bearing, clearly visible, the names of the three angels, the famous Senoy, Sansenoy and Semangelof, the only ones capable of overcoming and neutralizing Lilith. Perhaps they were observing all this from a distance. They had no reason to intervene, nobody had summoned them and they don't do volunteer work.

Even if their three names had been written out in full on the walls of my future parents' bedroom, even if to be absolutely sure there could be no mistake, they'd drawn the three weird birds said to represent them, it would probably have been pointless. The bedroom was much too far from the concert hall where Lilith came for me.

Had she flown there in the guise of an owl, as it's said she likes to do? Or was she her usual self, a beautiful, winged demoness with long hair flowing all around her? Whichever, she was invisible to the humans she flew over as they listened to Beethoven. I didn't see her either, I simply felt her hands around my neck.

In the absence of an amulet, my mother could have armed herself with a few small parchment scrolls tied with string, like those given by Solomon of Troyes, known as

Rashi, to members of his community who asked him for talismans to protect them during a journey, an illness and, of course, childbirth. He would write one or two verses on the parchment. I'm glad to mention Rashi for two reasons: firstly, because I met him several times when I was living in Gan Eden, in the section for souls that had not yet been sent out. How come? Because he had obtained permission to visit the new little souls. In his lifetime, he had always been a curious spirit, and he had a great fondness for children. He loved to tell stories, beautiful rabbinical legends, so we adored his visits and celebrated him. This charming ancestor lived on earth, in Troyes, in Champagne, in the eleventh century. He was such a smiling, polite soul, always with a kind word, that I was delighted when I heard someone knowledgeable say that he was a distant—very distant—forebear of my future mother.

Among our ancestor's favorite verses were those from Psalm 91: "You will not fear the terror of the night, nor the arrow that flies by day, nor the pestilence that stalks in the darkness, nor the plague that destroys at midday."

Those verses are magnificent, but they are too general. It would undoubtedly have been better to have had a few scrolls inscribed with verses from the Bible that were specifically intended to protect women in childbirth, mothers and, above all, newborns. This one, for example:

"Now the Lord remembered Sarah as he had said, and the Lord did for Sarah as He had promised." But there you are. No one had thought of the little scrolls. And besides, I wasn't a newborn, strictly speaking. Of course, I was new. Let's say I was new but not born.

People will say: this baby who's not even born is much too smart, it's some kind of trick. But you must remember that I'm a soul, and a soul knows all manner of things which are instantly forgotten at birth. But I was not born, so I haven't forgotten anything.

The Rabbis maintain that souls were all created on the sixth day, at the precise moment when Adam, the first man, was created. The souls that have not yet been called upon reside in Gan Eden, where a section is reserved for them. This section is separate and even a little removed from where the souls that have already dwelt on earth live. When it is a soul's turn to be sent down to earth, or simply when the Eternal One feels like arranging the conception of a new mortal, He summons one of the angels responsible for guarding us and instructs him: "Bring me soul *Ploni*," which in Hebrew means "So-and-so" or "What's-his-name." Souls have a name, of course, but their name is only mentioned at this point and then never again. As for the soul, it forgets its name at the very moment of conception. So, in the stories told about the moment when the Eternal One decides to send a brand-new soul to earth, we say "Ploni." It's simpler. The angel immediately understands which soul it is and seeks it out. Most souls resist; they have no desire to leave Gan Eden, where they lead a rather pleasant life. But the so-and-so soul knows what's in store: the angel is going to stuff it into an embryo or even into a drop of sperm to save time and spare his efforts. In any case, the soul whose turn it is has no choice. The angel catches it, and bingo! into the embryo.

I have never seen the two ruby gates that lead to Paradise, so beautifully described by Rabbi Joshua ben Levi in his famous "Treatise on Gan Eden." Ploni souls aren't allowed to see the myriads of angels guarding these two gates, whose faces shine like the heavens. Nor do they see the righteous who enter through these gates, clothed in garments made of clouds of glory, and wearing two crowns, one of precious stones and the other of pure gold, as they are led to a place where streams babble and eight hundred species of roses and myrtles grow. I have never seen the canopies of gold and pearls beneath which they are installed. I, little Ploni soul, only know all this from the detailed description given by dear Rabbi Joshua, who seems to have spent a long time under one of these canopies, sitting at his table made of precious stones and pearls, eating honey and sipping wine!

When the angel came to collect me, I put up a bit of a struggle. My friends made disgusted faces: "Poor you, you're going to be stuffed into a drop of sperm," but as he led me away, the angel tried to reassure me: "You're going to a great place! You're going to the Bronx! You're so lucky." Actually, I was only protesting because it was expected. You have to realize that not all Ploni souls are the same, some are better than others. I'm a soul of excellent quality, courageous and gifted with immense curiosity. I really wanted to go and see what was happening on earth. "Ciao, friends," I said cheerfully, "I'm off to the Bronx!"

And I found myself snug and warm in my mother's womb, guarded in turn by two vigilant and benevolent angels. The future looked bright. But that was without taking the demoness Lilith into account. On the night of the concert, the angel on duty fled at her approach, knowing that she was the stronger and that the battle was already lost.

Those who read the Talmud learn that the fetus sees from one end of the universe to the other. It sees the whole world, thanks to a candle that the angel Laila, whose name means night, lights and places right next to its face. Throughout the pregnancy, as the fetus grows, matures and develops, an angel teaches it the Torah. That doesn't just mean the books of the Bible. It means everything there is to teach, everything there is to know. Of course, the angels also talk about the baby's future, but there's one subject that's never mentioned. And that is whether the baby, once born, once grown up, will be righteous or wicked. It's a choice each person has to make.

The future human child receives a very thorough education. But at birth, the angel on duty gives it a little tap just above the mouth and it instantly forgets everything it has learnt. It is just a poor, ignorant baby who has no memory of those long hours spent learning. Just the imprint of the angel's finger above its top lip.

But remember, no angel had time to put his finger above my lip.

The day we came home from the hospital, they were all there—I say "we" because even though my body was already rotting in a garbage bin, I was still hovering around the pair who would never be my parents, but whom I still considered to be my parents. I couldn't abandon them as they returned to a life in which I would always be the tiny and yet huge absentee. So, that day, all the old ladies and the husbands who were still alive were waiting for us in front of the apartment building. It was a gathering that could only have been described as solemn. I recognized them by their voices, these people I was seeing for the first time, now that I was no longer in the womb, but a little soul flitting around my mother. Some people may not believe me, of course, but the fact is that a soul that flutters around people it is struggling to leave behind once and for all has very good eyesight.

The old ladies hadn't brought down their folding chairs, and none of the men had sat down on the steps of the building or on the low wall beside it. They just stood there, waiting.

No one was reading or commenting on the newspaper. Not one of the men even had his newspaper under his arm. "Look, little Isaac, look," my mother whispered, as if in a dream. "They've put on pretty frocks, like for a ceremony. Old Faegele is wearing her little hat with a veil."

They were waiting for us, my mother, my father and me, the absent baby, the dead hope. I recognized Joe and Selma right away, they looked exactly the way their voices had sounded to me: Joe, teeth clenched, looking mournful under his fedora, fat Selma, wig all askew and a warm, affectionate smile. "Dear Joe, dear Selma," whispered my mother. "They wanted to be the first to greet us. That doesn't surprise me." My mother was telling me everything, in a hushed voice, or rather, she was talking to herself and I could hear what she was saying.

Selma was clutching a plastic vase in which she'd placed a red rose. She handed it to my mother with a warm: "Welcome home."

Everything my mother said to herself, every idea that came to her, I could hear as well as if I'd still been snug in her belly. "Look at Shirley's hair," she thought. "So shiny and black, it looks like a helmet. She must have redyed it for the occasion. Some occasion!" And I, a little soul with excellent eyesight, could see her black hair gleaming in the sun. Max the truck driver stood beside his wife, arms dangling, the sparkle gone out of his eyes, an old giant whose strength was of no use.

I recognized Mr. Ruben, of course. It could only be him, in his immaculate light-grey suit. He had adopted a grave, respectful attitude, his old charmer's smile wiped off his face for once. There was no question that day of gratifying my mother with his usual: "Don't run, what's the hurry, what's the point?"

She wasn't running, poor thing, she wasn't in a hurry. In a hurry to go where? To an apartment where she had hoped for me and which would now be empty of that hope? In fact, she was walking very slowly. We were on our way back from the hospital on a glorious, almost summery morning, with blue skies and tender green trees, fragile and yet triumphant. The kind of morning that made Mrs. Feinberg whisper, in a voice that I had heard so often: "Yes, a beautiful day, of course, but since Hitler, the seasons have never been the same, you know."

There she was, tiny, drab and trembling, holding on to the arm of her husband who was barely taller than her. He was wearing the dark grey fedora that my mother said he never took off. In his grumpy voice, which was familiar to me because the Feinbergs lived next door to us, he mumbled two or three unintelligible words. And I agreed with my mother, who was thinking very loudly at that moment, so loud that it was deafening, that sad Mrs. Feinberg was right after all, and that the seasons would never be quite the same again. We were still a little way from Shirley, who was standing stock still, almost at attention beneath her shiny black helmet, when she opened her mouth and her thunderous "Welcome home!" rent the air, flying towards my mother. Tact was not Shirley's strong point, nor was silence. Several voices of varying timbres immediately echoed her: "Welcome home! Welcome home!" and then silence fell again. There was nothing more to say.

As for my mother, she didn't feel like talking to anyone but me. "Look, little Isaac, look," she said. "They're all here. If you'd come back in flesh and blood, swaddled up in the little blue blankets we'd already prepared, they'd all have been there, just the same, but happy and proud." I hovered beside her. It was all I could do.

My father parked the car, the little red Toyota that would never carry me again. My mother was walking slowly, numb, empty, clutching my absence to her breast with the plastic vase and the red rose, between two rows of elderly men and women with ravaged faces who were, on that day, our mourning tribe.

When my father joined us, Joe went ahead to open the hall door. Before stepping aside to let us pass, he raised a finger to the sky. Then, in an icy voice, his eyes filled with such dark anger that for an instant the world I was leaving was summed up for my mother and for me by that somber rebellion in old Joe's eyes, he said:

"You wonder what He's thinking of, Him up above. First He allows Auschwitz, and now this."

Over the next few days, Molly made a point of phoning every morning to console her daughter-in-law. She thought it was a shame, of course, but in any case, the baby wouldn't have been as adorable as her own son. That's debatable, I thought, outraged. I might have been much better, having acquired all sorts of very interesting chromosomes along the way. Besides, what a strange way of offering support. A bit weird, my ex-future grandmother.

But still, that was better than some letters of condolence. One in particular horrified my mother. "How lovely it was to talk to you and share your grief," wrote a vague friend who prided herself on her great sensitivity. "I now understand that when I grieve, I have to talk and cry with someone who doesn't try to console me. It's so good that you're able to express your pain and sorrow."

Then followed two long pages from this very sensitive person about her own ability to experience and analyze her pain.

Another very sensitive friend ended her letter by writing of her own grief when her cat had died a few months earlier.

"Can you believe it?" cried my mother, who was very fond of cats. She read these out to my father. And the letters, shredded into a thousand pieces, flew around the room and littered the floor.

Life had to go on. My mother went food shopping. The grocer, a Korean woman who always had a little chat with her customers, looked at my mother's flat stomach and her pretty, round, smooth face lit up.

"Baby?"

My mother replied, of course, that there was no baby.

The grocer burst into sudden and loud sobs. She sobbed for a few seconds. Then she quickly wiped her eyes with her sleeve, bowed deeply to my mother, straightened up, smiled at her and went back to putting vegetables in the bag.

Sam was heartbroken. He had already drawn up a list of all the things he could do with me. As well as the saxophone, he was going to teach me how to swim, skate, play baseball and, most importantly, how to gaze at the stars through a telescope on cold winter nights when the sky, even in New York, is incredibly clear.

"Take me far away from here," wailed my mother, the day after the concert, after the visit to the doctor who had been devastated as he told her that my heart was no longer beating. "Take me someplace where this nightmare isn't happening. Let's go, right now," she pleaded, clinging to my father, weeping. There was still hope, perhaps, and that hope was to flee and take refuge in a place where her little one's heart would regain its regular beat and the promise of life.

A few days later it had become: flee the place where Isaac André Gedalia had been murdered. Old Joe's words had remained imprinted on her mind, forever associated with the return from the hospital, associated with the moment when my absence had begun. Old Joe had been right. A little Isaac André Gedalia reduced to nothing, dead but not buried. Incinerated after being placed in a special garbage bin for small bodies fit only for incineration.

Obviously, a soul doesn't need to take a plane to travel, but I was still clinging to my mother. I went with her on the flight to Paris. Throughout the entire time, I stayed glued to her, snuggled up against her chest, so close to her that I could hear her innermost thoughts.

We were going to where it hadn't happened, where none of all that had happened—no Beethoven sonata, no asphyxiated baby, no demoness strangling unborn children.

By fleeing New York, my mother wanted to escape my absence. She didn't immediately realize that once she arrived in France, she'd have to establish that absence there too. I had already vacated the places in New York where my father pictured me—the planetarium, for example—as well as several places where Sam used to take him when he was a child, and where both of them had planned to take me. One day, I would also have to vanish from an utterly uninteresting neighborhood where I had brought such happiness to my parents for several months that my mother had come to see this mediocre Bronx neighborhood as her true home. I'd have to disappear from that not particularly pretty park where she'd tell me stories while watching the cars go by. But first I followed my mother to France with the mission of vacating yet more places she'd filled with my future presence, those where she'd seen me in her dreams, and where I'd never been.

Vacate the premises, little Isaac, yes, that's right. Remember. As soon as we arrived in Paris, we went to the Luxembourg Gardens, opposite the family apartment. For months, I'd been imagining you playing in the sandbox on a fine spring afternoon, wearing dungarees and armed with a pail and shovel. It was a very ordinary dream, nothing extravagant. I saw you getting off the pony on which you rode up and down the paths with other children on their ponies, proud as Artaban. I also saw you getting down from the white elephant with its cracked paintwork waiting for you as it spun tirelessly on the merry-go-round to the sound of the fairground organ. We had to take you away forever from the Luxembourg Gardens where I'd spent my childhood and adolescence, as did your big brother and, many years earlier, your grandfather André. From these Luxembourg Gardens that had been awaiting you too.

You and I also had to go to a village in the Sarthe and, once again, empty the place of your future presence. You had to leave the big grassy area by the river, pompously called the beach, and get off the slide and the swings. I wouldn't have let you swim, of course, just as I'd never allowed your brother to do more than wade in the brown water that smelled strongly of silt. All the same. I had to watch you get out of the water once and for all.

You had to stop swinging on the barn door, thrilled by the creaking of the old hinges. Finally, I had to persuade you, with so much grief, little Isaac, but I had no choice, to let yourself slide gently off the low wall of the little garden in front of the old house with its thick stone walls. You had to leave that low wall warmed by the summer sun where two generations of children from what was to be your family had been photographed sitting astride it, huddled together, cousins laughing, waiting for teatime.

I had to tear you away from these ancient yellow stones, overgrown with tufts of grass and crawling with lizards, which you will never have touched. You'll never have felt them, warm and rough in your child's palms. The stones that were supposed to be part of your heritage.

And so, little by little, I saw you remove yourself from various places, "as the sea withdraws at high tide, leaving here and there on the vast expanse of bare sand little pools that slowly evaporate in the sun." Those were the words that came to me one day. I'd written them down in a notebook. This poetic comparison, which was a little absurd in the circumstances, made me smile and yet it expressed exactly what I was feeling.

People full of good intentions and influenced by Eastern spirituality said to this poor mother who had so wanted to be mine: "Don't be so sad, don't say he's dead. Quite the opposite, he continues to exist. He simply decided not to come into the world, into your home, right now. You have to accept that. Come, don't cry, this child still exists, he's just chosen to be embodied elsewhere, in another family, in... in another... er... receptacle..." vaguely Buddhist friends would repeat over and over. "Another... sanctuary... another... situation..." they'd say, full of tact and anxious to find the right word, since "womb" sounded inappropriate in this spiritual context.

As consolation for one whose baby had died in violent convulsions during a concert, for one who hadn't realized what was happening and who would have given anything to prevent it, this hardly hit the mark.

"Another receptacle?" she yelled angrily.

As for me, I listened closely and found these conversations very interesting. So much so that gradually, being a self-centered little soul eager to experience life on earth among the living, despite the Beethoven that had left me with a nasty memory—but humans were not to blame for that—I started thinking that perhaps it was worth trying once again, rather than let myself be meekly transported back to the kindergarten of Gan Eden.

I have excellent memories of Gan Eden. It's a great place to make friends and have fun. You can bathe in a little pool of dew when the angels watching over you are otherwise occupied, because in principle that's not allowed: the dew is used to resurrect the dead. You can also watch the impressive frisbee matches between the angels. You should see how they swing the frisbees and then throw them vast distances, from one end of the world to the other! And what makes these matches such fun is that the frisbees are the souls of the wicked, condemned for eternity to serve as toys for the playful, energetic angels.

But I'm not Ploni anymore. If I went back to Gan Eden now, it would be a lot less fun, and I'd probably have to start studying.

"There's nothing to stop a little soul from having a taste for adventure," I told myself.

The Wanderings Of Isaac André Gedalia

In this "sanctuary," in this "receptacle" that I'd so reluctantly left, I'd felt myself developing various personality traits of two families who certainly did not lack the adaptability and curiosity that had already characterized me when I was merely Ploni.

A desire to travel, for a start. Even if, for the people I already considered to be my ancestors, travel had very often been synonymous with persecution and exile. Those whose names I was to bear had been expelled from various countries where they had lived in relative peace for a long time. André, the mathematician, was descended from people who had been driven out of Rostov-on-Don by the proverbial "little breeze of anti-Semitism." Gedalia had been forced to flee Ukraine. Having survived one pogrom, he had no wish to experience a second. Besides, for Gedalia and his brothers, it was a question of escaping the Tzar's army, where the Jews, forcibly conscripted, received nothing but ill-treatment.

A few decades later, André and his family also had to flee France, where they had thought they were safe, to avoid being put in cattle cars bound for Auschwitz. In the womb, I had been part of two families who had experienced hasty departures, leaving everything behind, goodbyes on station platforms or jetties, or in shabby, cold, grey hotel rooms in the early hours of the morning. My father's ancestors had trudged through dark forests with wives and children, having become undesirables in the country where they had grown up.

Was I not an exile too? I found myself exiled from a place where I had been happy and at peace for months before being attacked, suffocated and, in the end, not pushed out but forcibly removed.

"So, since I'm an exile, let's hit the road!" I said to myself.

For a while I didn't go anywhere. For how long, I don't know. A month maybe, or a year. I should tell you that for a little soul hovering around its parents—unwillingly torn away from them, even if that sounds strange—time doesn't exist. Then I wandered around a bit. I couldn't return to the Ploni section of Gan Eden. Even if I hadn't been born, I didn't really qualify as a new soul. Besides, all my playmates had left, selected one after the other to try their luck on earth.

I wanted to live, too. I wanted to be a baby being cradled and suckled, a toddler learning to walk, playing, falling, grazing its knee and being comforted by its mother or father. I wanted to fall asleep to the sound of human voices singing lullabies, I wanted to ride a bike and roller-skate. I wanted to feel the joy of warm, living arms around my living body. A little soul is so alone, people don't realize. I was a lonely little soul and, to tell the truth, despite the sense of humor that sets me apart from many other souls, I was sad. I wanted a mother!

So there came a time when the thirst for adventure that had been awakened in me by the words of my mother's friends became more pressing. And, since it was all about Eastern spirituality, I decided to start by taking myself off to Japan. It's not very difficult to travel when you're a little soul without any baggage, if you don't count as baggage my longing for the person I still considered to be my real mother. She'd been to Japan and was planning to return. She liked the country and was fascinated by its unfathomable nature. So it seemed to me that, by making this choice, I was in some way staying faithful to her.

When I arrived in Kyoto, I very quickly chose as my mother a woman called Mitsuko, a traditional, graceful name that indicated she probably came from a good family. Naturally, I wasn't going to trust just anyone to give birth to me. She was from Sendai. She'd been married for a short time, a passionate, whirlwind love match. She was happy and wanted a child. She wanted a boy she would call Yoshihisa, a distinguished name—you could almost say noble—since the kanji character Yoshi means splendid and excellent, and Hisa, permanent and eternal. I was thrilled at the idea of having such a name. Also, I could tell that Mitsuko had a very affectionate nature.

Little did I know that this idyllic situation would soon turn into a rather bizarre drama, which I shall recount as best I can.

On a beautiful spring afternoon, someone sitting in Kyoto's smartest tearoom would have observed a soberly dressed woman, outwardly very calm, not looking around, not smiling at her neighbors, not rummaging in her bag, not doing any of the things that lone women often do to keep up appearances. She was simply waiting. I was just a tiny spinal column, or a rather large grain of rice concealed in her flat, athletic belly, waiting with her.

I go back to that moment because it's a fateful one, and I don't want to gloss over it for those who might be interested in this story. So, in the tearoom, at that fateful moment, my mother-to-be, Mitsuko Fujiwara, wife of the highly respected dermatologist Dr. Fujiwara, is waiting. When the cake arrives on a small plate, she bows her head to thank the waitress but doesn't say a word. Same thing when the waitress brings the bowl containing the matcha. She gazes for a while at the slightly irregularly shaped ceramic bowl, and also at the cake.

A barely perceptible smile plays on her lips. Finally she raises the bowl, places it on the palm of her left hand, supporting it with her right hand, and gives it a quarter turn clockwise. She takes two sips, with a slowness that seems studied. Then she examines her cake: a soft pink petal, a delicately rounded cherry-blossom petal made of bean paste. She hesitates before cutting it with the kuromoji, the small wooden knife. A work of art like this has to be cut not only in the proper way, but also in the most aesthetically pleasing way.

I can guess her every move, just from the way she breathes. I can sense the slightest change. I'm a particularly alert little soul, remember.

My mother-to-be is tall, rather heavily built for a Japanese woman. Her face is a beautiful, impenetrable mask. She is solemn, as if reflecting. Her silence is louder than the voices of the three elegant women sitting nearby, chattering away as they savor the traditional snack of sweet bean soup, louder even than their muffled laughter and their "Ah so desu-ka!," louder even than the cawing of the crows—hundreds of them on the branches of the trees.

In the past, the tea master would prepare the matcha for the warrior about to go into battle. I, the grain of rice nestling in Mitsuko's belly, had just gained a certainty: both tea master and warrior, calm and resolute, the proud Mitsuko was silently indulging in her own solitary tea ceremony. She sought and found her strength in the matcha. Enclosing the warm, smooth bowl in her hands, gazing into the opaque, dark-green liquid, she was gathering her wits, scattered by surprise, grief and humiliation.

Three days earlier, Fujiwara-san—the doctor's mother—and her son had spent the evening alone, Mitsuko having gone to visit her parents in Sendai. Fujiwara-san waited for her son, who had just returned from the gym to take his bath. She placed a small dish of salted vegetables and a bowl of creamy tofu seasoned with soy sauce in front of him. This was followed by the vegetable and fish tempura that he had loved since childhood. Finally, she served him a bowl of very thick, very sweet red bean soup. This is his favorite dessert, as he obviously never has time to eat this soup in the middle of the afternoon. Fujiwara-san poured the tea, watching her son eat. Then, taking her time, she said, in a quiet but firm voice:

"I can't bear to live with her anymore. She's got a mind of her own. She rides roughshod over my habits, which are your habits too. One of us will have to leave this house."

After a brief silence, she added: "I can go and live with my sister."

The highly respected doctor hesitates. An only child, he has lived with his mother for forty years. My future mother, on the other hand, has only been with him for two months. He married her for love but hasn't had time to become deeply attached to her. He's thinking about his career, which would suffer from having to deal with an impossible domestic conflict. He wants time. To think things over.

He bows to his mother and says:

"I am guilty. I behaved impulsively. I should never have forced this situation on you."

They couldn't know that Mitsuko had taken the train back from Sendai earlier than planned. Not yet feeling comfortable enough in her mother-in-law's house to announce her return, she went in without shouting the conventional joyous: "I'm home!" She gently closed the door, took off her shoes and walked in without making a sound.

They never realized that she had heard everything. I'd heard everything too. She went up to her room without saying hello to her husband and mother-in-law.

Nothing happened for a few days. The doctor was very busy. He was probably hoping that things would settle down on their own. At any rate, he was putting off an unpleasant conversation until later. The young Mrs. Fujiwara stayed in the house as little as possible. She went shopping and had tea. Isolated, a little lost in this city that was not her own, she reflected on her strange situation. Sometimes she cried. Doctor Fujiwara had been her first true love.

Back at the house, alone in her room, stretched out on the tatami mat, tired—I'd begun to give a few subtle signs of my existence—sad and mortified, she wondered what she had done that so displeased her husband's respectable mother.

And I, the grain of rice, felt sorry for her and worried about her future, which was also mine. The position of the wife of a brilliant doctor in a city like Kyoto was rather enviable. I didn't think the brilliant doctor was very nice, but that didn't matter. This was Japan and Mitsuko would have brought me up, not him. Divorced, my poor future mother was more or less condemned to become one of the countless office workers, dressed in the regulation black or navy blue suit, who squeeze into the Metro at rush hour. An ant! An ant with a child who, at the time we're talking about, the 1980s, had no chance of having a successful career. And I had no wish to be the son of an ant.

Her mother or grandmother should have explained to her how easy it is for a wife to fall foul of her mother-in-law. Especially when it's a love marriage, because in such cases no one asked the respectable mother-in-law for her opinion. To give herself the best chance of success, the bride must understand from day one that she is only a guest in the house where her mother-in-law remains the absolute mistress.

So, it was easy to fall foul of a mother-in-law. First of all, it was impossible for Mitsuko, who was almost a head taller than Fujiwara-san, to make herself look small in front of her. Mitsuko was proud of her height. Hadn't she been chosen to be one of the hostesses at the Dermatological Association conference in Sendai precisely because of her statuesque looks and good manners? Didn't Dr. Yutaro Fujiwara, hardly a passionate man, fall head over heels in love with this tall, reserved woman with a perfectly smooth oval face and beautiful eyes? It was such a lightning romance that the wedding took place barely a month later!

When they returned from their honeymoon—a week in Hawaii—real life began. On the first morning, Mitsuko rose early and went into the kitchen. She decided to prepare miso soup. First, she peeled a potato and sliced it. She was following the recipe of her grandmother, who loved potatoes and had no qualms about adding them to her soup, even when she wasn't making taro imoni, so popular in Sendai. In her eagerness to do well, she had forgotten that her grandmother was an eccentric character and that putting potato in miso was a peasant custom! Then she started cutting the daikon, the radish, into long thin strips, imitating the precise movements of her mother and especially her grandmother.

She was so absorbed in her task that she didn't see Fujiwara-san come in, and her courteous but sharp voice made Mitsuko almost drop her knife.

"It's very kind of you to want to help me in the kitchen, but that's not how we cut daikon in my family. We cut it into half-moons, which is much prettier. And never, ever, do we put potatoes in miso soup."

Fujiwara-san went on in a kinder voice: "You should have asked me how to do it."

Mitsuko bowed.

"I apologize, I didn't realize."

"From now on, you must call me Okaa-san. Mother."

Mitsuko bowed silently this time. She was far too proud to show that she was on the verge of tears. It felt to her as if her beloved mother and grandmother had just been insulted, considered as undesirables, uneducated bumpkins to be sent back to Sendai where they belonged.

A few days went by. Mitsuko rarely went into the kitchen. She was content to serve her husband and mother-in-law at mealtimes. She didn't seem the least bit curious about the Fujiwara family's culinary traditions. She spoke to her mother-in-law in an infinitely respectful tone, of course, but did not call her Mother, which showed an annoying lack of submission.

One morning, as she was serving him his soup, the doctor looked up at his young wife and smiled at her in a happy, knowing way. Mitsuko, leaning towards him, also smiled. This amorous look only lasted a second, but Fujiwara-san was disgusted by it. As soon as her son disappeared into his surgery, she called Mitsuko.

"Earlier, I couldn't help witnessing indecent behavior which is inappropriate in a respectable house. If my son has had an enjoyable night, so much the better, but it should not be obvious. It is up to the wife to set the tone, right from the start."

Mitsuko turned bright red. She bowed deeply several times.

"I'm sorry, I apologize, and I thank you for your advice."

As for me, I'd just moved in, the result of that night the brilliant doctor was so pleased with. Nobody suspected, of course. What was perfectly clear to Fujiwara-san, however, was that for all Mitsuko's bowing and apologies, everyday manifestations of everyday manners, the young Mrs. Fujiwara refused to submit.

A few weeks went past. Mitsuko decided to go and visit her parents in Sendai. From where she returned a few hours earlier than planned.

Now aware of her new family's feelings towards her, a mother-in-law who couldn't stand her and a husband who didn't care enough about her to defend her, my future mother, a young woman from a good family, was humiliated. She thought her husband might well consider divorcing her rather than displease his mother. It has been known to happen. Every morning she leaves the big, square, yellow-plastered house to walk briskly along the flat banks of the river Kamo-gawa. Sometimes she stops to watch a heron, standing motionless on one leg and looking about him with a round, undecided eye. Will she remain undecided, like the motionless heron, or will she leave of her own accord, without waiting to be dismissed like an unsatisfactory servant?

So it is that in Kyoto's smartest tearoom, on a beautiful early spring afternoon, a tall young woman with a beautiful, inscrutable face is performing a tea ceremony alone and drinking matcha like a warrior preparing for battle.

Fate was to intervene in her favor. A few days after the conversation overheard by Mitsuko, my future grandmother collapsed in her kitchen. She was probably cutting her radish into little half-moons. An ambulance was called and Mitsuko accompanied her mother-in-law to the hospital. She was diagnosed with diabetes.

Fujiwara-san was to spend several weeks in the hospital. Since the single rooms were all occupied, she was put in a beautiful, spacious room with five other ladies.

On the first day, Mitsuko sat at her bedside. She read aloud to her from an article about gardens in England. She read very well and her voice was sweet.

On the second day, the young woman asked her mother-in-law:

"Your neighbor, Tanaka-san, came to ask after you. She's very worried and will be back this evening. What exactly would you like me to tell her and the others in the neighborhood? I'd like to make sure I do as you say."

On the third day, she was at the patient's bedside when the injection was given. The nurse, a small woman with quick and efficient movements, called Fujiwara-san "Fujiwara no Obaa-chan." Grandmother Fujiwara! and she used the most familiar form! Mitsuko could see straight away, from her mother-in-law's suddenly downcast eyes and averted face, that this forwardness offended and displeased her. She stood up, bowed deeply to the nurse, rose to her full height and said loudly:

"Saito-san, please tell me whether my mother-in-law had a good night. Any discomfort? We're very worried about her!"

The nurse understood. She too bowed, and answered:

"Fujiwara-san slept well. Don't hesitate to call me if you need anything, Fujiwara-san."

That evening, Fujiwara-san's fellow patients congratulated her. How lucky you are to have such an attentive daughter-in-law!

My future grandmother fell asleep very content, her head full of pleasant thoughts. She's lucky, she has a daughter-in-law who earns her compliments. The next day, she was delighted to see Mitsuko arrive. She was carrying a voluminous bag containing several illustrated magazines and also the bean-filled pillow on which Mrs. Fujiwara usually rested her head when she slept.

Mitsuko bowed to her mother-in-law.

"I thought you'd get better faster if you had your own pillow here."

One afternoon, at the beginning of the second week, after greeting her and asking her how she was feeling, Mitsuko said:

"Forgive me for bothering you with my questions, but I can see that, despite my best efforts, I'm not able to prepare the sweet red bean soup exactly the way Yutaro-san likes it.

He didn't say anything, but it was obvious that he didn't like my soup."

Fujiwara-san smiled and dictated the recipe to Mitsuko, who thanked her by smiling too. Meanwhile, as a curious and perceptive little soul, but not perceptive enough to understand Mitsuko's plan, I had been wondering all along where this was leading. For as my mother-to-be smiled, I was well placed to feel the extreme tension in every one of her nerves. It appeared to me that I was witnessing a strange duel between the two people in the world destined to be the closest relatives of the future Yoshihisa. Me.

Fujiwara-san regained her strength. Every afternoon, Mitsuko arrived promptly when the doors opened for visitors. And every afternoon she started the conversation like this:

"I apologize for tiring you with my questions, but since you've left, Yutaro-san doesn't seem very happy with his dinner. I'm doing my best, but if you could give me a few pointers…"

Or else:

"As you know, Yutaro-san never comes back for dinner at the same time. I can't manage to serve him his meal straight away. If you could give me some advice..."

Or again:

"Last night Yutaro-san came back very late from a doctors' meeting, he was drunk, which is perfectly normal, I don't blame him, but if you could tell me how to behave when this happens..."

Every evening, after Mitsuko's departure, Fujiwara-san was showered with compliments. "You must be so proud of your daughter-in-law. Pretty, devoted, respectful. You're so lucky!"

One of her fellow patients said:

"My daughter-in-law is very nice, but you could see that she thought she'd done enough when she stayed with me for fifteen minutes and brought me a fan or a bottle of eau de cologne."

Another laughed:

"My son will surely marry one day but I will never be happy with my daughter-in-law because she'll never measure up to yours! How lucky you are!"

And they all exclaimed in unison:

"Fujiwara-san was born under a lucky star!"

How did I know about these conversations? They were repeated, more or less word for word, to Mitsuko the minute she arrived. In the eyes of everyone at the hospital, Fujiwara-san was a very important person. Of course, she belonged to one of the best families in Kyoto, but above all, she was the lady at whose bedside sat, for hours on end every day, a tall and beautiful young woman, submissive and obedient, her daughter-in-law.

Dr. Fujiwara visited his mother from time to time. She remarked that he looked well, despite his very busy days with his expanding practice and professional meetings. There was talk of him being elected vice-president of the Dermatological Association.

One day in the third week, as the sun was shining brightly in the big white room, Mitsuko suggested that her mother-in-law take a walk in the hospital garden on her arm.

"It's a very mild day, Okaa-sama, I think it will do you good."

Fujiwara-san thought she'd misheard. Okaa-sama! The most respectful word in the Japanese language for Mother!

And I, who had now grown to the size of a rather large bean, was wondering how all this was going to turn out.

That afternoon, as they walked slowly through the hospital garden, Mitsuko explained that she was dispirited because she realized that she wasn't able to keep the house at all as her husband would have wanted. My future grandmother had a moment of perfect happiness. She replied, in a kind and even affectionate tone:

"You'll soon learn. I'll advise you."

At the end of the visit, Mitsuko thanked her profusely, with a deep bow and an Okaa-sama that her neighbors couldn't fail to hear. Fujiwara-san was overjoyed.

The day finally arrived when the doctor came to collect his mother from the hospital. Mitsuko had stayed at home to get everything ready. A gentle spring breeze was blowing, the cherry trees were in full bloom, and even the crows' squawking sounded like squawks of joy. I imagined Fujiwara-san, sitting in her son's very comfortable car, watching the familiar streets of her old Kyoto go by, and envisioning a bright future. She tells her son that it would be a good idea to modernize the house, to make it a bit bigger, why not? When she gets out of the car, she is surprised not to see

Mitsuko rushing to greet her. The doctor says she must be cooking something special, she's been making so much effort lately. He laughs. Fujiwara-san smiles. They go inside and announce themselves. No answer. No footsteps.

Just as her husband and mother-in-law entered the yellow-plastered house, just as they discovered a veritable spring feast waiting for them on the beautifully laid table decorated with cherry branches, Mitsuko was on a train heading for Tokyo, her forehead pressed against the window. She was feeling very tired. The final act had been performed. The sun was setting. I was about to leave.

And suddenly, not far from Mitsuko, and therefore from me, a very old voice whispered with reverence: "Fuji-san, Fuji-san." I felt Mitsuko straighten up and look up at Mount Fuji, majestic in its perfection, almost menacing, dark against a violently pink sky. Beside us, the quavering voice, hoarse with emotion, repeated: "Fuji-san, Fuji-san." I imagined wrinkled cheeks with tears streaming down. The old man was probably not surprised to see Mitsuko burst into tears as Mount Fuji vanished into the distance. But it wasn't Fuji she was crying over, it was me, because she had just felt that I was leaving her. I hadn't even been there two months, I was only a centimeter and a half long. I was just the beginnings of a dream. Mitsuko hadn't yet had time to imagine the child I'd become, to imagine her Yoshihisa, an over-indulged toddler, following Japanese custom, poking his nose and fingers in everything, then one day, when he was about seven, magically transforming into a well-behaved and studious schoolboy in the regulation blue blazer. As for the unobservant dermatologist, he had seen nothing and guessed nothing. The discreet Mitsuko hadn't said a word to anyone.

It was a fairly easy departure. Medieval medical manuals claim that miscarriages can be caused by "movements of the soul" such as anger, spite or sorrow. The same manuals refer to "working too hard." The task of playing the perfect daughter-in-law to a selfish and cold mother-in-law could be described as too hard a job. As waves shake a boat without necessarily capsizing it, anger, spite and sadness jostled and shook up the future little Yoshihisa. Me. Yet, instead of giving in so quickly and running away, I could have hung on, held out and waited to see how things would end.

Why didn't I take a little longer to decide my future? Because, while remembering my origins, I had inevitably become a somewhat Japanese little soul when I'd chosen Mitsuko as my mother. I knew, therefore, that an unborn or stillborn child must be punished for the grief its death has caused its parents. No more than I could see myself as the son of an ant could I envisage spending a chunk of eternity on the banks of the river Sanzu, which is a horrible, stony river, in the company of other unborns condemned to carry stones to build towers that would allow them to reach a more pleasant afterlife. And these towers, of course, are quickly demolished by terrible demons, forcing the little souls to start all over again. Not to mention the fact that the demons take great pleasure in beating up any little souls they manage to catch.

These are very ancient beliefs, but they are still widely held in Japan. Now, since I had become a slightly Japanese little soul, I thought that this Sanzu River might exist somewhere. So I chose to slip away as quickly as possible before I was noticed and selected for the job of transporting pebbles along the desolate banks known as Sai no Kawara.

As for the woman who was no longer my future mother, I had the impression on the train that she was determined to leave Kyoto for good, after dreaming up that original and cruel revenge. The dermatologist could remarry twenty times, his mother was doomed to miss Mitsuko until the end of her days.

A garden filled with plants and flowers adjoining one of Kyoto's temples. A tall, beautiful young woman who had almost been my mother walked purposefully towards a section crammed with several hundred white figurines. As if she had an appointment. Visibly emotional and without a moment's hesitation, she went over to one of them: it was the Jizo Bosatsu that she had entrusted to watch over me, the unborn Yoshihisa. She recognized this statuette as easily as my French mother in New York had recognized the white bubble that was her unborn Isaac. She could have had a bigger, more beautiful figurine in a special section of the garden by making a substantial donation to the temple, but she didn't feel the need. Even from a distance, Mitsuko could see "her" jizo standing among hundreds of almost identical white statuettes, with their large round heads and red hats and bibs. Some of them were wearing make-up, pink blusher on their cheeks and lipstick, a vulgarity to which Mitsuko would never have consented.

She squatted in front of the statuette for a long time, crying a little, straightening the hat she herself had knitted and smoothing the bib. As she did so, she caressed the white, slightly rough cheek of the stone jizo, as she would have done that of a living child in a stroller. The red hat and bib were supposed to keep the demons away from the jizo and make it easier for him to protect me. Then she took some pebbles out of her bag and piled them up in front of the jizo. Some mothers had put toys in front of "their" jizo, as well as biscuits and other treats. Mitsuko promised herself she'd bring some next time. That day, all she had were pebbles, but that was the main thing. The pebbles were to make my job easier, since my beloved, affectionate Mitsuko imagined her child condemned to building towers.

As she piled up the pebbles, she talked to me and to the jizo, who is the protector of travelers, but especially of children, unborn children. She begged him to come to the rescue of the little soul, Yoshihisa, who was trapped on the stony banks, and to save him from the demons' violence, to conceal him in his wide sleeves and take him to Paradise. She had ordered and paid for a number of mizuko kuyo at the temple—services to commemorate the "water children," the unborn. It was during the first ceremony that she put an inscription on the back of the jizo statuette, making it hers. She had organized all this on her own, because the mizuko kuyo is a private, individual and often secret ceremony. You don't join other bereaved mothers.

I would have liked to make my poor Japanese mother Mitsuko understand that I was still there with her, that I hadn't been sent to the stony banks of the river Sanzu. I hovered around her, close to her. I did my best to make my presence felt. I wanted to console her a little. As you will have long realized, I am a loving and faithful soul and I feel infinite sorrow at being separated from my future mothers.

I must finally confess here that I was mistaken. For a little soul of such excellent quality, I had been short-sighted because, in the end, I would not have been the son of an ant. Mitsuko had chosen the most convenient solution, and undoubtedly the most Japanese. She went to her family for a week's rest before taking the train back to Kyoto. On the advice of her parents, she phoned to explain that she had been called urgently to Sendai to visit her sick mother. She had been too upset even to leave a note on the table. All in all, it was a happy ending: the mother-in-law adored her daughter-in-law, showered her with gifts, encouraged her to be friends with women of the same social class and to take music lessons while awaiting the birth of a little Yoshihisa who would not be me.

But Mitsuko, faithful and loving soul that she was, like me, had not forgotten the first future little Yoshihisa, even though he'd never grown bigger than a bean, and she still mourned him in secret.

I didn't try to find another Japanese mother. Another failure might send me to join the little souls condemned to build piles of stones. This time, my hasty departure had allowed me to escape the unhappy shores of the Sanzu River and I considered myself lucky.

On reflection, I also decided not to embark on any more exotic adventures. You'll recall that I was to be named not only Isaac, but also Gedalia in memory of a very pious grandfather who lived in Brooklyn, and whose prayer shawl my mother regularly aired. She didn't think it was silly or ridiculous to make me admire it and the tefillin—the phylacteries—of grandfather Gedalia, even though I was still in the womb. Those names, which should have been mine during my first life as a human being, had left their mark on the new little soul that I was then. You could say that I had roots in Brooklyn, if a soul has roots, that is. But no one can accuse me of not having tried something else. I could have been born Yoshihisa, the son of a brilliant dermatologist in Kyoto, and been raised on the shores of the river Kamo-gawa.

In Brooklyn's Hasidic neighborhood, there was a woman called Neshama who greatly intrigued me. I'd heard of her, back when I was just a Ploni soul. People would say: "Ah yes, she's quite a character. She travels the world in search of her dream husband!" The search for a spouse is a very ordinary activity for human beings, but for Neshama this quest was a real passion that had occupied and preoccupied her for years. That's why she was talked about in Gan Eden.

She had just turned thirty and was finally engaged. I found her story touching. She'd been looking for a husband much the way I, a lonely but demanding little soul, was looking for a mother. We were alike.

A Ploni soul doesn't choose the family it will end up in. But I wasn't Ploni anymore. I'd been around a bit and known a number of very different humans. I was curious to see the man that Neshama (her name boded well since it means soul and there I was, a little *neshama*) had finally found.

She'd gone to so much trouble, poor thing. She had travelled all over the place: Belgium, France, England, Israel... She had undergone, yes, undergone, that's the right word, a hundred shidduchim, meetings with a view to marriage. And what meetings! She'd find herself in a matchmaker's kitchen, sitting at the end of a very long table covered with an ugly oilcloth, while at the other end was a man. Needless to say, this man had been described by the matchmaker in the most glowing terms: he was already a partner in his father's firm and would eventually be running their very prosperous household appliance business; he didn't smoke, or he smoked very little. Or he was a very conscientious boy who studied Torah all day long, had spent a year in a yeshiva in Jerusalem, not to mention the fact that at least two of his great-grandfathers had been famous rabbis in Poland... In front of Neshama, a can of Coke. In front of the young man, a can of Coke.

The descendant of the Polish rabbis looked at Neshama, took a sip or two of Coke, and finally asked her what kind of furniture she'd like in her living room. The conversation dragged on for a few minutes, Neshama said goodbye to the matchmaker and left. The future director of the very prosperous company described for a quarter of an hour, without stopping for breath, the pleasant life he would be able to provide for his future wife. Another descendant of several rabbis stared suspiciously at the young woman for a long time before telling her that the day before he had gone to buy a coffee machine in her father's shop and that her father had been wearing a blue shirt. "A truly pious Jew doesn't wear a blue shirt," he declared peremptorily. Neshama fled without even saying goodbye to the matchmaker.

It was hard for her to find a match. She came from a family considered eccentric in the neighborhood. Her father, who owned a fine hardware store, claimed to be a direct descendant of Rashi. He had decreed that his children would receive a modern education, not just religious instruction. He allowed them to take music lessons. He chatted with customers, sneered at hypocrites and dressed as he pleased. He did not get along well with his wife and readily said that he would have preferred a less religious and more intellectual wife.

Neshama wanted a husband who would be a friend. "*We're* your friends," said the young women she knew, who were more realistic and had been married for years. "A husband is a husband, not a friend," they repeated to Neshama, who, stubborn as a mule, wanted a friend.

So, in the end, who did she choose? A neighborhood guy whom she'd known for a long time and who wasn't a Hasid but had promised to adapt. He would learn Yiddish and grow his beard, which was a lovely light ginger.

The first time she saw Shalom, they were both in their twenties. On Sundays he worked as an assistant to a photographer who specialized in wedding photos. "The minute I set eyes on him," she told her friends, "I felt that my soul, my neshama, was drawn to him. I felt our souls were connected."

She had seen Shalom several times at weddings. She couldn't take her eyes off him. From the front, he was quite handsome, but from behind, he gave the impression of a person who was broken. He was hunched. Neshama thought to herself: this boy needs a word of encouragement. She felt like patting him on the back, as one does a small child. He needed affection. But with his clean-shaven cheeks and his little modern kippa, he didn't look at all religious. She wanted to talk to him but hesitated. She confided her dilemma to a friend. The friend was adamant: "If you go and talk to him, you'll marry him. Do you want to marry this boy, just because he needs affection, because he's had a difficult childhood?"

"No, of course not," replied Neshama. and then she wondered what girl would want a boy who, so young, already seemed broken. So she said a little prayer, softly: "This boy needs a little help. I'd like to talk to him but I can't. Please, Hashem, comfort him, take care of him."

And then one day, after so many years of seeing each other at weddings, one of Neshama's friends, who didn't want Shalom as a husband but thought he was nice, arranged a "meeting." Shalom and Neshama sat opposite each other at the kitchen table of Neshama's older brother and soon, after a long walk in the Brooklyn Botanic Gardens, they got engaged. For my part, I was certain that Neshama would be an excellent mother, loving and attentive.

While I waited for Neshama to get married and for me to move in with her, I drifted around the neighborhood. I was drawn to a certain café that was considered chic and highly suitable for first dates. It was far less off-putting than the kitchen table of a sister-in-law or matchmaker. The atmosphere was pleasant and intended to be "Parisian." One of the walls showed a view of Paris with a huge Eiffel Tower in the center. Isaac André Gedalia, who was somewhat French, would surely have had the opportunity to visit that famous landmark. So I floated leisurely in front of the "Parisian landscape" and watched, like a curious little soul, as young couples staked their future in this seemingly innocuous setting.

And then, one cold, dreary winter afternoon when there was snow in the air, I felt drawn to one of those couples. It was Nahum and Myriam.

They had ordered ice creams. She had strawberry. He chose vanilla. They watched each other in silence. The boy's fine features clearly showed his displeasure at wasting, here in a tearoom, beneath a ceiling imitating a softly muted blue sky, hours that he'd rather have spent studying. They began to eat their ice creams. The girl tried hard to suppress a fit of nervous giggles. Too late. He had noticed and his forehead creased with annoyance. And so, certain that she couldn't displease him any more than she already had, she decided to speak first, in defiance of convention. She took the plunge:

"My older brother is studying at the yeshiva on Seventeenth Avenue." Success! The boy's tense face had lit up: he looked like a person who's nearly drowned and having risen back up to the surface, sucks in a great gulp of air. He put down his spoon.

"So what part is he on?"

"What part?"

"In the Talmud. What tractate is he studying?"

She, poor thing, had to admit that she had no idea. She added, by way of apology:

"I hardly ever see him. He's always learning."

Her triumph was short-lived. In front of her, against a backdrop of the Eiffel Tower and overgrown lawns, the boy's face had clouded. When she asked him if he had any sisters, she already knew the answer: he had four brothers, no sisters. She noticed he was sweating. He grasped his hat, pushed it back, then pulled it back down over his forehead. He wiped his brow furtively with the back of his hand.

She wanted to show him that she was less stupid and more educated than many other girls, and that she was determined to continue learning. She would have told him that she'd studied the reading for the week, with the Song of the Sea and even Rashi's commentary explaining that the Egyptians got stuck in the sand of the Red Sea which had turned to mud because the Lord wanted to repay the Egyptians in kind for having reduced Israel to slavery and made them work with clay and bricks. She didn't dare. He, of course, had reached a much higher level of knowledge and interpretation. He would have had nothing but contempt for her childish babblings. She cast about for something else:

"It will soon be Passover. My uncle and aunt are coming from Montreal. They have ten children."

It must have been one of the demons responsible for wrecking these kinds of dates that prompted her to add:

"Men can't imagine how much work it is for women. Cleaning the house, getting rid of the leaven. Shopping. Cooking. My mother does it a month in advance and every year she ends up exhausted. But I help her."

None of this interested the young man who was not destined ever to clean a house or cook meals and whose face was now closed, locked for good. He smoothed his beard with a disgruntled air. Was she some kind of rebel? Some kind of feminist? The demon had won.

The poor feminist blushed and squirmed. Perspiration streamed down her back and her brand-new red jumper scratched and irritated her skin. She said, very quickly, without conviction:

"All the same, Pesach is the most beautiful of festivals. He led us out of Egypt with a mighty hand."

And then nothing.

I really liked those two and I was having fun. Two children. I was so much older than them. I snuggled right up to them to understand them better, to feel what they were feeling. I could feel them sweating, I could sense their panic and the efforts they were making to hide it!

She ate a spoonful of ice cream. So did he. She watched the way he put the spoon in his mouth, the way his lips moved. She noticed that they were full and looked soft. The man's cheeks, although not very pink, weren't sallow like those of some of the men she saw in the street hurrying to yeshivot and synagogues.

As he sucked his spoonful of ice cream, she could tell that he'd withdrawn into his own thoughts, into his boyish world, and that he couldn't wait to get back to his books, later helping his little brothers with their homework, perhaps playing ball with them for a few minutes in front of the house while waiting for dinner.

She imagined the conversation—and I imagined it too—that evening, at the dinner table, between Nahum and his mother.

"She's not as pretty as she looks in the photo? What's wrong with her?"

"Pretty or not, I don't like her. She's a chatterbox who started by making fun of me and then she wouldn't stop talking and I have nothing to say to her."

The mother would burst out:

"Nothing to say to her? That's the limit! You, the top of your class, more knowledgeable about Talmud than the rest of your classmates put together, you've got nothing to say to her? Didn't you mention that with your business acumen, one day you'd be able to offer your wife a very comfortable life? Didn't you ask her what kind of house she'd like? What style of furniture? That's what marriageable girls are interested in."

He would sigh, tired but happy to have gained time. His mother would sigh too. She'd say, with a chuckle:

"If I can't find anyone in the neighborhood, I'll have to go online."

"Whatever you want. And I'll talk house, furniture, dishware, silverware. But find me another one."

Myriam was upset. Then the Almighty came to her rescue. He sent her an idea. An inspiration. And she said:

"Let's not speak any more. Let's have a staring contest."

Now that's an original idea, I thought. I was having a very good time. Young Nahum could have refused. Said that it was late, that he had to go, that he'd walk her home. But he didn't. Perhaps he'd remembered, as she had at that moment, that the eyes are the mirror of the soul. What they didn't realize was the presence of a wandering, curious little soul, who was very interested in the outcome of this game the girl had just suggested.

First, their eyes had to seek each other out, meet and lock. It's hard for the eyes to settle on someone else's gaze, to stay put, to adjust. His eyes tried to flee. She caught them and forced them to return. He blinked desperately. He moved his head forward, then back.

She too was blinking, but more slowly. Now their gazes were locked. No more tugging. The ice cream in the bowls began to melt. The vanilla. The strawberry.

The boy's eyes are brown, dark brown, opaque but warm. They are still a little astonished, slightly wide open, but already his eyebrows are relaxing, letting go, no longer acting as barriers. His eyes, freed, question. Scrutinize. Without malice.

She knows that her eyes are beautiful, an unusual color, a very light hazel, almost transparent, with hints of green. She too relaxes. She can no longer feel her hands, which were tense with anxiety just now, or the knot in her stomach. She is aware only of her eyes, resting on the brown, almost black eyes that have entered the game in earnest and now bear the weight of her own eyes without flinching, with no ulterior motive, open and honest.

The ice creams had melted, creamy pools at the bottom of the metal bowls. Their gazes remained glued, fixed, locked together, immersed in each other. Leaning forward, in turn smiling and serious, frankly happy, on the verge of tears, dizzy and dazzled, breathing the same breath, their eyelids beating to the same rhythm, until they became afraid to stop. Afraid of the cold that would grip them the moment their gazes let go.

They got married just before Passover, just as the first crocuses were appearing in the gardens. And I, enchanted, forgetting about Neshama I'm ashamed to say, moved in with them right away.

They were a nice little couple. He was still studious but in love with his wife, and she took her role as housewife very seriously, making it a point of honor never to cook the same dish twice in a row, but spending several hours a week at the local library where she read psychology magazines. She was interested in child psychology. But then, after three or four weeks, I got the distinct impression that I was going to be a girl. A catastrophe. I'd spend my childhood looking after a string of little brothers and sisters, while waiting to get married to produce another string. I would have been called Rivka, or Deborah-Dvorka in memory of a great-aunt who died in Auschwitz. Deborah means bee, I would have been a hard-working and fertile bee. No thank you. I had to hurry and leave before the demons realized I was there.

When I'm the one who decides to leave, it's not very difficult. I took the opportunity to slip away at a wedding where Myriam, herself a happy and enthusiastic bride, shook me right out by dancing wild horas with her sisters, cousins and their friends. Not too much damage, a very slight disappointment from which Myriam would recover all the faster as a brand new soul was certainly waiting in the wings to come and take the place I'd left. As for me, as you can see, I'm a little soul full of contradictions. And stubborn. I want to live, but as soon as I don't like a situation, I bail out.

Out of ideas, I foolishly rushed to Neshama's, married just a fortnight ago, but I arrived too late, the place was already occupied. There was nothing to stop me from waiting and being Neshama and Shalom's second child or continuing to search. The world has no shortage of very welcoming families: normal, reassuring and boring families, strange, amusing families, families of all kinds.

But, in the end, the ties that bound me to my scattered-about Bronx mother were too strong, and I felt an irresistible urge to return home, quite simply. To find the people I'd never stopped thinking of as my real parents. It had been two or three years in human time, I think, since I'd left them. They were still living in the Bronx.

My mother had no idea that it was me again, or rather the idea had crossed her mind from the start but was immediately dismissed as too ridiculous. Once or twice, all the same, she had asked herself the question, could it be that… Return, reincarnation… We were so deeply bound, she and I. But no. It went without saying that I would be a different child. We had to give a chance to this other child, who would have a different name and who would perhaps be a girl. Those were happy weeks. Four, maybe five, no more. It was lovely to hear all the familiar voices again. I'd missed them. Molly, who would soon be complaining that my mother couldn't stand onions anymore, and Sam, still talking about his saxophone. The voices of old Joe and fat Selma. Mrs. Feinberg's weak and exhausted voice. I was back home. I felt the joy of one who has returned from exile, but it was a joy filled with anxiety. Can you really come back? Had I been right to come back? I was no longer a new soul, far from it, but I would forget my wanderings at the moment of my birth. It was worth the attempt.

My mother didn't even have time to think about choosing names. One afternoon, while she was attending a colleague's lecture on Marguerite Duras's *The Lover*, I felt myself being pinched and pulled, a tiny defenseless bean, with just the beginnings of extremities, my future arms and legs. I was torn from the soft warm chamber where I'd nestled, dragged away by a small torrent and carried towards the exit. Which low-ranking demon had persecuted and killed me this time? Lilith would never have deigned to come in person for a bean. Drowned in the toilet, flushed away. The attempt had been expelled.

I went back into exile. My scattered-about mother in the Bronx was obviously forbidden to me by demons or rather by a misfortune that I only understood later. But I was tired of wandering, disheartened, because even a little soul gets tired and disheartened. I travelled to the children's section of Gan Eden. The Archangel Metatron, who exercises a number of important functions, including those of Chief Scribe and High Priest of the Celestial Temple, teaches us the Torah. I study and play with other children's souls. We have beautiful lawns and all sorts of fruit trees. But I very regularly take a few moments out, especially on the date that would have been my birthday, to go and be with the one who will be my real mother for all eternity. The mother of Isaac André Gedalia.

The day I should have celebrated my twenty-fourth birthday if I hadn't been asphyxiated by enemy hands while my mother was listening to a Beethoven sonata—you could say I'm dwelling on it, that I haven't moved on, but it's not the kind of event you forget easily and put behind you, as the psychologists say, it's even the main event of my life as a little soul and I've never really got over it, especially because I haven't managed to recycle myself satisfactorily despite several attempts—so, the day I turned twenty-four, I went to spend the day with my mother, as I do every year, on that birthday that was never celebrated.

It was just before this twenty-fourth birthday, or perhaps just after, or the following year, that my mother received—and so did I—some news that we could have done without. It was a real blow, a terrible humiliation.

Is it possible? What was it all about? Well, it turns out that it wasn't Lilith after all. And yet, when I think of that ill-fated concert, I can still feel the demoness's ruthless hands around the neck that was mine at the time.

It wasn't fate either. My mother had reconciled herself to the idea: she and I had been victims of Fate. A victim of Fate is necessarily noble, joining the ranks of the very talkative and eloquent heroes of Greek tragedy.

One day, then, my mother learned that it was a mutation that caused the blood clot. No destiny, no malevolent jealous demons determined to prevent humans' happiness—in this case the very human parents who were so thrilled to be mine—and deprive them of offspring. Just a little blood mutation, neither jealous nor malevolent but utterly indifferent and completely uninteresting. As for Lilith's strangling hands... Nonsense! It was blood clots that had suffocated me. What could be more mundane, more common than a blood clot? We found ourselves desolate, defeated, empty-handed. With no consolation.

It wasn't the lack of amulets that was to blame. It was the absence of what now takes their place. Pills are today's amulets, pills of all shapes and colors. Every morning with a glass of water, a tiny little pill, a pretty pink or green or yellow pill, and that's it: no Lilith, never heard of her, Fate goes after someone else, a baby is born. In any case, for us, this scientific breakthrough came too late.

My mother was filled with a crushing silence. A horrified silence. Which lasted a long time. Days and days. Perhaps weeks. Years.

Let's go back to the day of my non-celebrated twenty-fourth birthday. That day, my mother had gone looking for a church on the banks of the Ourcq Canal in Paris. I joined her.

By the way, some people might imagine that when I join her, I perch on her shoulder like a tame monkey, but they'd be mistaken. That's not the way a little soul moves about. First, I flutter around her a little, then I come closer, I snuggle up to her and I stay like that, clinging to her, listening to her. On that day, my birthday, all her thoughts were directed towards me and enveloped me, even those that had nothing to do with me.

Yes, little Isaac, with you, this morning, with you so close to me even after so many years, I got out of the Métro after a long ride in a crowded train to find myself on a sidewalk surrounded by a colorful throng. I walked past shop windows full of cheap merchandise. I felt like I was very far away. So far away that it was no longer avenue de Flandre but an avenue running through the Bronx where, twenty-four years ago, a child died before he was even born. You. Today, or perhaps yesterday or tomorrow, you would have been about the age of a young man I'm very fond of who, the day before yesterday, wept as he told me that his grandfather had died in Cuzco.

She who had passionately wanted to be your mother, little Isaac, was running to a church she didn't know, grieving for a grandfather she didn't know, grieving for a young man the age you would be. Grieving for you. He had lost his grandfather. But you had lost everything.

I walked along the avenue de Flandre to the corner of the rue de Crimée. I was disoriented, far from home. I was looking for the Ourcq Canal. More precisely, I was looking for a church by the canal and I had no time to lose. I had to get there on time, I owed it to the young man I'd heard crying on the phone, so I hurried, out of breath, distraught that I didn't know where the church was.

When I was little, my favorite toy was the kaleidoscope. It was, of course, the ideal toy for a child scattered about too soon and very much against her will. You too, little Isaac, I'm sure you would have loved it. I'd have given you one for your fifth birthday. And now, in the prism of my imaginary kaleidoscope, buildings and shops were disintegrating, multiplying, separating and coming back together. Passersby were dancing. The kaleidoscope turned a little, the buildings pivoted, became upright again, rue de Crimée broke into fragments then put itself together again and it was another avenue in the Bronx.

At first, I was disappointed. What had I been waiting for? A neighborhood like the ones Simenon describes so vividly, little old ladies with their shopping bags, gossips, standing around in their slippers, whose glances speak volumes, cafés where men in caps drink red wine, leaning on the bar? Totally old-fashioned. Since I was looking for the Ourcq Canal, it was probably the word "canal" that evoked those images. But the truth, little Isaac, is that walking along rue de Crimée, she who so wanted to be your mother was telling herself that reality is twofold, that there are almost always two superimposed pictures. So, on rue de Crimée, I could clearly see a street in the Bronx, and I felt both sorrow, a sorrow that was nothing new, and a kind of joy. It was a strange, unexpected way of sensing your presence near me.

I had no time to lose. I went up to a woman who was neither old nor young, probably Chinese, quite short, carrying a colorful waxed canvas shopping bag, a modern version of Simenon's little old lady's shopping bag. That's what drew me to her. Reassured me. Just by saying "shopping bag" I feel as if I'm giving a little twist to the kaleidoscope, the scenery turns a fraction and I see my mother coming back from the market carrying an old navy blue shopping bag. I thought to myself, this woman is shopping, she's from around here. I asked her, *"S'il vous plaît, madame, le canal de l'Ourcq?"* But she shook her head in panic, mumbled "No, no..." a few times, and then walked away as fast as her short legs and shopping bag full of vegetables would allow. A man was coming out of a café. Possibly also Chinese. I went up to him. He at least smiled at me and replied: "Don't know it." I repeated: canal, river? A church? and he kindly said: "Canal, church, don't know it."

A youngish man to whom I asked my question, "*Pardon, monsieur, le canal de l'Ourcq?*" had no idea either, even though he didn't look like a tourist.

Where were the gossips who knew everything, the locals who could tell me? I seemed to be surrounded by a bunch of extras dropped by helicopter, at the junction of avenue de Flandre and rue de Crimée, precisely to create the impression of a neighborhood. They were part of the backdrop.

An awning advertised Breton crêpes. I headed for the crêperie. A young man no more Breton than me was making crêpes. Breton crêpes. I started the conversation very politely, as with the others, Excuse me, sir, et cetera...

"Canal?" he muttered while spreading Nutella on a pancake. No. He shook his head. I insisted, a bridge, a river, water... In desperation, I even made a swimming gesture. He kept shaking his head, canal, river, no. I started shouting, "So you're here all day but you don't know anything about the area and you don't give a damn, you don't even know there's a canal, quays, a bridge, a church... the only thing you're interested in is your crêpe batter and spreading your Nutella!"

I was beside myself. All this has nothing to do with you, but it has everything to do with you, with your absence, your eternal absence, it's blindingly obvious, and today, little Isaac, would have been your birthday and you'd be grown up. Not little. And you would have already lost your four grandparents. You'd have come with me to this Mass for the Peruvian grandfather. Yes, of course you would have come with me.

The young crêpe-seller looked at me a little taken aback, but not that much. He too was an extra helicoptered in. Breton crêpes are a nice "neighborhood" touch. His role was clear: he was there to spread Nutella on pancakes, not to answer questions from a stray passerby. He wasn't interested in the Ourcq Canal. I was sickened. I turned my back on him.

I was going to be late. It was too stupid. At that moment, like a beacon on the pavement opposite, I sighted a dark silhouette, an extra who had been helicoptered in by mistake or had been brought from the Bronx to confirm my illusion. Black suit, a bit of a paunch, big black hat, grey beard. A velvet bag under his arm: his tallith and tefillin, of course.

He was in animated conversation with a ponytailed man wearing a green tank top. Surely not his future son-in-law. An employee, perhaps. The man in the black hat, perhaps put there by mistake, was part of a scenario that was familiar to me. At least I knew what was on his mind: he had business in hand and he wanted to marry off his daughter, the shadchan had found a desirable match in Brooklyn or Buenos Aires, the meeting had to be arranged, and he would still find time in the evening to study a few pages of Talmud. Out of necessity, he would have learned geography and would know where the Ourcq Canal was. I was not disappointed. He even knew the church.

The little chapel where the Mass is held looks more like a classroom. Nondescript. A bit dingy. A sort of pulpit in the center serves as an altar. An elderly man in a worn jacket enters the chapel. He's carrying a stack of prayer books. Is he the priest? I know the Church has modernized and this is not a High Mass, but I'm horribly disappointed. It would be very unfair to the grandfather who died over there in Cuzco. To honor him and also to honor his grandson who's so far from home, I want a priest dressed in a real chasuble embroidered with gold thread. I want a real ceremony.

The elderly man puts down his books and leaves. Ha! It was only the sacristan. We wait in silence. The few rows of chairs have filled up with old ladies who must also be extras, hired to fill the chapel, or maybe real parishioners who attend midday Mass every day. Now I'm back in my Simenon novel. Thin, neat old ladies, not exactly elegant but showing no signs of poverty. They know what's going on in the neighborhood. They glance discreetly at our exotic battalion. They're probably used to Masses for Peruvian grandfathers.

What a relief to see a real priest finally come in, dressed as befits. Green and gold chasuble. He's even older than the sacristan, and speaks slowly, addressing no one in particular. He must be on tranquilizers. He reads a passage from the Bible, the daily reading, that of the day I'm passing through, what a coincidence, and on your birthday. He's got it right, the old priest on tranquilizers, his monotonous, sleepy voice wakes me up with a jolt. He's reading the passage about Abraham and Sarah. She will conceive and give birth at the age of ninety. The child will be called Isaac because she laughed. I too was expecting a little Isaac, I too had laughed. And you would be twenty-four today, or perhaps tomorrow.

 The old ladies sang two or three not very beautiful hymns, and the Mass ended. Now, at the home of the bereaved man, we're eating pizza, watching a small screen showing a long, endless column of men marching through a jungle. Dragging guns and horses, in silence because the sound is muted, sometimes climbing rocky slopes, sometimes wading through muddy waters, metal helmets polished and shiny or disheveled hair, ponchos and armor, they trudge along, following Klaus Kinski with his magnificent, bitter mouth and crazy blue eyes. Someone pauses the film on a close-up. A group of men and also a woman, standing in a jungle. Some very straight, stiff, helmeted, wearing armor. The others are rather ragged. They look grim. To Kinski's left is a handsome, dignified man holding a halberd. His beard, mustache and eyebrows are very black. He's wearing armor. The film starts up again, the characters continue plodding through their jungle, then another close-up on the same man who's now holding his halberd in his other hand. Attentive, tragic, he leans forward a little to look at Kinski.

The man we're looking at now, little Isaac, the man with the halberd whose solemn, noble face freezes in close-up on the screen, is a grandfather who died three days ago in Cuzco. He was part of my life, because he was the grandfather of the young husband of the daughter of the second wife of my first husband who is the father of your big brother. It's a family situation that I've always considered to be normal, just a little complicated.

We have another slice of pizza and gaze at the beautiful face of the grandfather with the halberd on the screen. And you, you would have been twenty-four years old and you are and always will be little Isaac, and you will never have another face than the one you had on the ultrasound images.

Those horrible, touching images, that little innocent, delicate profile, similar to all the little profiles of seven-month-old fetuses—who does he look like, he looks like everybody, like anybody, André, Gedalia, Molly, it's anyone's guess. Anyone's dream. He'll be good-natured, he'll be ill-tempered. I ended up throwing out those images, as you know. It took years for me to decide to tear them up and then throw them away. Yes, forgive me, you've been thrown into the bin once more. I couldn't stand looking at that face-that-wasn't-a-face that forever reminded me that you would never have one.

No, no, no, little Isaac, don't listen to them. You didn't die the victim of a common blood clot. I know that you died a hero, I do, that you resisted, fought with all your strength to vanquish a demon who wanted to prevent you from living and bringing life and also descendants to your parents. The clot is the explanation for the others, for the idiots who believe in blood clots because they don't understand anything. You fought Lilith like a true hero.

In front of the basin filled with little white bubbles, just when I was officially reunited with you at last and I called you by your name, a memory came back to me. One day, when I was in the Luxembourg Gardens with your grandfather André, and we were walking in silence, and slowly, the way he now walked because he'd become old and a little bent over, he stopped abruptly and raised his head to say to me: "In the end, you and I had a good life, we didn't go to Auschwitz."

And, without thinking that one had nothing to do with the other, I replied: "But I had a dead child." For me, little

Isaac, it had everything to do, I never stopped considering your death as a murder. You had been murdered.

And now, sweet innocent little white bubble, I call you once more, one last time, by your three names and I bid you farewell. Farewell Isaac André Gedalia.

END

About the Author

Sylvie Weil has published several novels and collections of short stories, as well as several books for young adults. *Le Mazal d'Elvina* (*My Guardian Angel*) won the prestigious Prix Sorcières in France and was named a Sydney Taylor Award Honor Book in the U.S.A. Her critically acclaimed memoir *Chez les Weil* (*At Home with André and Simone Weil*, Northwestern University Press, 2010) was translated and published in several languages. Her book *Selfies*, published in Paris in 2015, was translated into English by Ros Schwartz (Les Fugitives, London, 2019).

About the Translator

Since 1981 Ros Schwartz has translated some 100 fiction and non-fiction titles from French, including *Selfies* by Sylvie Weil. In 2010 she published a new translation of Antoine de Saint-Exupéry's *The Little Prince*, and she is currently one of the team retranslating George Simenon's œuvre for Penguin Classics. In 2009, she was made a Chevalier de l'Ordre des Arts et des Lettres. Ros gives talks, workshops and masterclasses around the world and is co-director of Bristol Translates literary translation summer school.